HAVE
YOU
GOT THE
WHY
"Y"
FACTOR

SHARING THE GIFT OF HEALTH, HAPPINESS AND WEALTH

AYO OLASEINDE

Copyright © Ayo Olaseinde 2014.

Published by Why Factor Academy LTD

ISBN-13: 978-1494927981

ISBN-10: 1494927985

Editing, interior design, and preparation for publishing by Action Wealth Publishing.

DEDICATION

This book is dedicated to my mother, **Edith Martha Olaseinde**.

She taught me the price of love, the price of commitment, she taught me how to deal with failure and disappointment, how to smile in the face of adversity, how to be an optimist. She gave me great principles and values to live by, and that has been the foundation of my success.

You are the best Mother in the world... I Love You.

My determination for success was to make sure the sacrifices you made for your children were not in vain.

We love you and miss you.

ACKNOWLEDGEMENTS

I first of all would like to thank my Father for his discipline. Also for teaching me how to be an optimist, and for my Christian upbringing.

My children, Joshua, Hannah and Lisa; for their love, support, putting up with me and for being my inspiration. You are the best; I love you and thank you for reminding me of the Why question.

A special thank you to my brother Dele Olaseinde and my Niece Yetunde Olaseinde for specifically composing, writing, performing and recording an amazing motivational song to go with the theme of the book "why not me". Yes look out for "Why not me" song in the charts.

I would also like to thank one of my main mentors in business when I was starting out; Mr. Gene Windfelt, Chairman and CEO of Preferred Credit Inc. Gene you made a difference.

The next person I would like to thank doesn't even know the role he played. I met him once; he was introduced to me by Gene and through his CD program he has been a great mentor. Mr. Brian Tracy, Chairman and CEO of Brian Tracy International. Brian thank you for your wisdom, education and coaching.

The same applies to Mr. Anthony Robbins, life coach, self-help author and motivational speaker. Tony, I have walked the fire walk twice. Thank you for unleashing the power within. Also, Ernie Villanueva, Jim Rohn, Nightingale Connaught and many more.

Thank you to Paul Middleborough for recruiting me and his excellent sales training in my early days.

I would also like to give a massive thank you to the Direct Sales Industry for providing a platform with programs and opportunities to take ordinary people like myself, believe in them and turn them into extra ordinary people; by coaching, educating and motivating people from zero to Hero. I am proud to be part of this Industry.

I would like to thank Mr Keith Peterson, President of Saladmaster, for his support and belief in me, the vice Presidents and executive team, Shirley Loutzenhiser, Gary Robinson, Mark George, Pidoy Pacis, Ryan Reigle, Rick Heath, the Regional managers, all at Saladmaster Headquarters, Jeff Reigle and the Reigle family.

I would also like to acknowledge a great team that i have the honour and privilege of leading, the UK , Ireland, African, European, Saladmaster Rhino Region Dealers, Distributors and Consultants. Also my Head office staff. You are an Amazing team to work with..... Thank you .

Lastly Geoffrey Semaganda and his team for all the help behind the scenes putting *The Why Factor* together.

As you can see success is Teamwork, make sure you pick your right team for success.

TABLE OF
CONTENTS

HAVE YOU GOT THE WHY FACTOR?

First of all, welcome to the Why Factor Academy. My system for achieving a healthy, successful and positive lifestyle is nothing new. Instead the Why Factor relies on a characteristic within us that has been around since the beginning of time, asking the "Why?" question. Think about when you were a child or when you are with your children. Our kids are constantly asking the question... "Why?" When we were children, we constantly asked our parents, teachers the question, "Why?" You would get an answer and then you would ask the question

"Why?" one, two, three, four, five times, "Why?" until your parents, teachers got angry with you and told you to stop being silly. This then becomes the point where you realise that asking the "Why?" question is not a good thing to do. As we drift through life, we tend to stop asking this simple yet powerful question. By re-introducing the question "Why?" into our daily lives, we can develop a better understanding of life and learn to build a happier, positive and more successful way of life.

WHAT HAPPENED TO MY WHY FACTOR?

"Why?" is one of the most powerful questions you can ask yourself if you use it positively.

For example "Why are some people more successful than others?" "Why are some people happier than others?"

By constantly asking myself the question, "Why?" I have enjoyed tremendous success. For me, the moment which changed my life involved working as a casual labourer in a bakery. I started to ask myself the question, "Why?" "Why am I stuck in the life I am currently living?" This was my life at the age of 24. Now, I am a successful businessman who has built an organisation that has turned over 300 million dollars of merchandise through my past and current business venture. The question I am asking myself now is, "Why have I not reached a £ Billion yet?" Simply put, by re-introducing the question "Why?" into my life, I have been able to achieve tremendous success, both professionally and personally.

You see, the journey of the Why Factor starts with humble beginnings, and leads to powerful and complex versions of the question "Why?" By managing these powerful and complex questions correctly, I have become a very successful businessman. But the journey is not complete. In fact, it is never complete. I am always asking myself the question, "Why?" which continues to make me more successful from month to month, year to year. For this reason, I feel compelled to share my story and lifestyle management system through the Why Factor Academy.

To start, we need to determine if you fit within the Why Factor Academy. With this said, not everyone is meant to succeed through the Why Factor Academy; I have learnt that **you can't help people who don't want to be helped**. In fact, there was a time in my life when I was certainly not ready for the Why Factor Academy. In many ways, in my younger years, I would have failed my own course! Or, I would not have been willing to learn or able to relate to the simplicity of the question, "Why?"

Learning How to Succeed and Learning How to Help Others

Beyond helping yourself, it is important to help others within the Why Factor Academy. This is especially true as we become more successful in life. We should all feel the duty to help others achieve happiness and success in their lives. By doing this, we enrich ourselves and we enrich our surroundings. In many ways, I decided to share my story, both the successes and failures, so that you may relate and achieve the same sort of success and hopefully surpass what I have achieved. Since I have helped myself in many ways, it is important for me to help others as it is one of the greatest gifts you could give; helping to change someone's life. To me, helping yourself and helping others is an integral part of a happy, successful and meaningful life and is part of our purpose in life...helping others.

One of the basic actions you need to take in order to succeed within the Why Factor Academy is *learning* how to become successful. Success is not just about wealth, success in your relationships with people, your partner, success in health, happiness, successful habits, being a successful parent. The list goes on. **Success is defined in the UK Oxford Dictionary as the achievement of something designed, planned or attempted.** Once you learn to become successful on your own, you can learn how to help others. First you have to accept the responsibility for your success. As you become more successful, you need to realise that many people have taken the time to help you succeed too. It might be a teacher, mentor, co-worker or your partner. Since many people will help you to achieve greater success, it is important to share your fortunes with the world. In other words, you need to return the favour to society, your family and friends. As we become more successful, we help ourselves, and when we help others, we help society. This shared social responsibility will make the world a better place. For this reason, the Why Factor hopes to help you, and it hopes to help society by teaching you to help others.

Through this process, we can build a better world.

While I will discuss many strategies and tips within this book, there is one very important step you need to take outside the bounds of this guide. In other words, in order to become successful, you need to be *open minded and willing to learn.* A lot of people do not know how to learn correctly. So, it is important that you always consider what steps you need to take to learn and educate yourself correctly.

If you want to find a new way to get somewhere in your life, you need to study which new road or path you want to go down. You might need to ask the question, what sort of qualifications will I need to reach my goals? Sometimes, you need to go back to school, while other times, you might need to gain more practical experience. In a sense, you need to develop a map of your successful path. Next, you need to make positive decisions in order to reach your goals of success. But to choose the correct path, you need to ask yourself, "Where am I now and where do I want to go?" "What do I need to do to change my path?" If you don't learn life's lessons, you will come full circle and find yourself in the same place, encountering the same challenges, again and again. **Life is a great teacher when you learn from your experiences.** So, it is important to be honest with yourself when it comes to your learning curve. Not just initially, but it is important to reflect on where you are in your journey of your life at all times.

It's like using your GPS Satellite Navigation System, first it needs to know where you are, and then it needs to know the destination. Then it will work out two or three routes and you will choose the one you want. Once it starts, it is constantly reviewing where you are and where you need to go next to get to your destination, and so it is with your life. You need to have a destination and review where you are at today and constantly be reviewing where you are in your journey to success.

Secondly, you need to learn **where** to find the correct information to learn your lessons. For instance, consider the scenario of a lazy Sunday drive. As you go through the day, you might get lost and find the need to ask someone for directions. Many times, the person who you ask for driving directions will not provide great directions because they too don't know the area well enough, and may send you to a place rather far from your desired location. First of all, you cannot blame that person for the bad directions. You need to blame yourself. You did not qualify the person giving you the directions, so you need to take responsibility for not asking the proper person for directions. The crime is when you keep on repeating the same mistake, for then you are not learning. **One definition of insanity is to continue doing what is not working for you but believe and expect that you will get a different result.**

"WHEN WILL YOU REALISE YOU ARE GOING DOWN A DEAD END ROAD"

Instead of just blindly asking a stranger for directions, the first question you might want to ask them is: "Are you local?" This is the best way to find a qualified direction finder. By framing the direction question in this manner, you have learned to ask the correct question, in order to get the correct answer. So, in order to learn correctly, you need to compose a game plan, and part of that game plan is in asking: who are the qualified people that can correctly help you with the problem of the challenge at hand.

Another analogy involves a plumber. If you have plumbing problems, you don't call a solicitor for help. You ask an expert with the proper credentials and training. So, when it comes to seeking assistance or advice on any situation or issue, make sure you gain advice from a qualified source.

Learning correctly involves asking yourself "Why?" questions often. In other words, you need to constantly question yourself positively, as well as question your actions. For instance, "Is my roadmap working in the way I had expected? Yes or No?" Then ask the "Why?"question. Or, "Have I reached my short term goals? Yes or No", then ask the

"Why?" question again. These are the sort of questions which will help you find the path to learning correctly. As we will discuss later in this book, it is important to study success and failure. Why are some people successful and why do some people fail? Constantly asking yourself "Why?" leads to learning what has led to your success and what learning that has led to your failures. By being honest with yourself and asking the correct questions, you will learn to identify who is a qualified source of information, and who is not and should be ignored.

With this said, it is always important to keep in mind that no one is stuck in their current state or position, especially when it comes to learning. Instead, you just need to go back to the books, audios and seminars and study. You need to learn how to research the topics which are relevant to your own path to success as well as how and where to find credible information. Within the Why Factor, we will cover these topics in great depth. In the meantime, remember this simple expression: **to earn more you have to learn more**.

The fact that you are reading this book tells me that you are special and unique and I want to commend you for taking the time to invest in your life to make it first class.

Four Types of People

In terms of categorizing people, I have concluded that there are four types of people in the world. The first group of people are the people who say "Why, Why Me?" These are the people who feel sorry for themselves and blame others for their problems. They live by the Law of Accident, it's never their fault, it's always someone else's, etc. This is a topic which we will discuss in depth later.

The next group of people are the people who ask the question, "Why, Why Not Me?" Technically speaking, there are two types of "Why, Why Not Me?" people. The first group of people have the ability to succeed, big ego, but do not act on their abilities. The other group of "Why Not Me?" people are the people who have the ability to succeed and do act on it. As you can imagine, this second group of "Why, Why Not Me?" people are highly successful. These are the people who realise they need to act in order to succeed. This impressive group of people realise what they want in life, and have the discipline to achieve their goals. They search for information and find the correct path to success. In many ways, these people are you. By joining the Why Factor, you have taken two of the most important steps when it comes to building a successful life. First, you have to make a decision that you need help and second, you need to take a powerful, positive action in order to do something about it: the two most important qualities you need in order to succeed in the Why Factor Academy. **Make a decision, take action on it.**

The fourth group of people, and the most unfortunate type of people, are the drifters. I like to call this group of people, the Wanderers. These people tend to drift through life like a herd of cattle, just drifting from job to job, day to day. My intention is to not be derogative to anyone, and it is important to remember that I have found myself in all four groups at some point in my life, in fact we can move in and out of the four categories. I started in the wandering stage, went to the "Why, Why Me?" phase, then onto the "Why, Why Not Me?" phase. Finally, I learned to take responsibility and to act on my dreams and desires, and became the active "Why, Why Not Me?" person. I can do anything I put my mind to, nobody is better than me, they are just ahead of me.

The Why? Why Me? People

Let's take a look at the different types of people. There are a few common traits of the "Why, Why Me?" people. You see, instead of acting to resolve their problems, they get stuck in a rut and can never seem to dig their way out of the problem. These tend to be the people who see the glass as being half empty. The "Why, Why Me?" people live a life of pessimism, assuming that the worst which can go wrong, will go wrong.

The "Why, Why Me?" people tend to be the negative people in the world. They see the world through depressing expressions such as, "Why do I always seem to draw the short straw?" Instead of looking at the positives of the world, they focus solely on the negative.

WHY ME? WHY HAVE I DRAWN THE SHORT STRAW?

When entering the Why Factor Academy, you need to be aware of these traits and make sure you abandon the things in your life which cause you to ask such negative questions. Instead, the active "Why, Why Not Me?" people are the ones who refuse to live with their misery. You see, misery is one of the unfortunate traits of the "Why, Why Me?" mentality and will hold you back.

The "Why, Why Not Me?" People

As mentioned briefly before, there are two types of "Why, Why Not Me?" people. The first group of people have the ability to succeed, but do not act on their abilities. This group of "Why, Why Not Me?" people feel they deserve everything but don't have a plan to accomplish their goals. They do not want to go the extra mile and work for their success. They tend to have great talent and abilities, big egos, but lack the discipline and drive to see their work become a reality and success. With this said, these are the people who can become actively successful, provided they add discipline and focus to their daily lives. The extra discipline and focus needed is discussed in great detail within the Why Factor Academy.

The other group of "Why, Why Not Me?" active people are the people who have the ability to become successful, and act on their desire to become successful. They are the highly disciplined members of the world, who understand that nobody is better than them but some people are ahead of them. They understand the hard work and commitment needed to achieve their goals. They are the group of people who truly know how to be honest with themselves. This group is well suited for the Why Factor Academy. The people within this active group of "Why, Why Not Me?" people are highly successful; both professionally and personally, and they are always using the "Why?" questions in a positive light. These are the people who realise they need to act in order to succeed, and have the discipline and work ethic to follow through and achieve their goals. They know how to search for information and find the correct path to success. They know how to ask themselves deep questions and be truthful with themselves. The "Why, Why Not Me?" active people believe in themselves. They actively find a way to achieve their goals and dreams, and have the discipline to stay the course and stay focused, even when pressures mount during their journey. **Life is truly a never ending journey of evolving to be the best 'you', you can be.**

The Wanderers

The saddest, most unfortunate group of people in the world are the people who never ask themselves the question, "Why?" They never question where they are in their lives or if they do, they just accept it. Instead, they simply tend to wander through life with a certain degree of ignorant bliss and avoid looking in the mirror. Some wanderers drift through life from childhood 'till the day they find themselves being placed in the grave. Again I am not being derogatory, I once was a wanderer, and in fact society and education teaches us that this is acceptable. We are products of our environment and acquaintances. Other times, a wanderer reaches a point in life where they ask themselves the question, "Why, Why Me?" It's still not a great place to be in life, but at least it's a step up from the wanderer stage. Sometimes, a wanderer finally reaches the point of being tired of drifting from job to job or day to day or relationship to relationship. Other times, a wanderer is forced to change because of some tragedy, death in the family, work redundancy, divorce and so on. From these unfortunate events, they ask themselves the question, "Why, Why Me?" In time, they may ask the question, "Why, Why Not Me?" With this question, they begin the process of changing and starting to take action. They stop accepting their circumstances and start to create a new positive perspective on life. In a sense, they become a member of the Why Factor Academy. Remember, this is a path I experienced, starting as a teenager, and ending with the person you see today.

WHY BE DIFFERENT, JUST GO WITH THE FLOW.

The Elephant and the Banyan Tree

In fact, this reminds me of a story I was once told when I was first starting out by my boss, Paul, who is now a good friend. The story was about how they trained elephants many years ago. When they caught a baby elephant they would tie a chain around its leg and attach it to a Banyan tree, which had deep roots and was very strong. The elephant would pull and pull to try and run away and eventually the chains would cut into the elephant's leg and became sore and bloody. The elephant continued until one day it was in so much pain, it gave up trying to escape. The spirit of the elephant was broken and the elephant would accept that there was no point in trying anymore, as it would never escape. From that day on all they had to do was tie a rope around the elephants leg and attach it to a little peg in the ground, once the elephant felt a little pull on its leg realising it had been through the process before with the chains and the pain, it would say to itself, "no point,

I've tried and I can't break free," and give up. You have this large elephant that can walk through walls and its' spirit has been broken: and so it is with us as human beings. We are like the elephant, we are strong, we can do anything we want to do but, because we have had some bad experiences, we give up and wander. Well I am here to tell you to take the rope off, cut the chains that are holding you back, it's time to start believing in yourself and realise your true potential. Let's do it... Why not you? Yes, why not you? Let's use the Why Factor academy to realise the amazing potential and greatness you were born with.

WHY ARE SOME PEOPLE MORE SUCCESSFUL THAN OTHERS?

When you enter the Why Factor Academy, you need to spend time learning from successful people and also learning from failures. One important question you need to ask yourself is: "Why are some people more successful than others?" By asking this question, and researching the answer, you will find a lot of helpful advice in order to become successful yourself, but most importantly you begin to realise that

nobody is better than you, they are just more skilled, rehearsed and doing things that you are not doing. In other words, **success can be learnt, it is not a gift.**

Some people are more successful than others for one simple reason: they work harder to achieve their success. Beyond working hard, successful people know how to learn from their failures and move on, they know how to use the Why question for success. They know how to be honest with themselves, and they know when it's time to make a serious change in their lives and have the discipline to follow through. These are just a few examples of why these people are more successful. For this reason, you need to pay close attention to the qualities and characteristics of very successful people.

The Different Shades of Success

Success is important in the Why Factor Academy. It is important to recognise that there are many shades and styles of success. For some, success might be measured by being elected to the House of Commons. For others, success might be measured by living their dream of opening a successful restaurant, or being a successful parent, etc. Many people judge success in terms of how their lives compare to the success of their parents. Finally, many people judge their own successes by studying the most successful people within their desired field or profession. For this reason, it is important to determine what shade of success you hope to achieve in your life. **True success is not competing with everyone but competing with yourself**... what are you capable of achieving?

To me, anyone can achieve anything in life within reason. However, you need to remember to select obtainable goals. If you are fifty years old, becoming a Premier League football star is not a realistic measure of success. Instead, you need to be honest about the goals you can achieve. You need to understand what goals are obtainable, both in terms of time and cost. For this reason, I like to think that there are many different shades of success. Just make sure to choose a level of success which is healthy and obtainable. We will discuss this concept in great detail as we move through this book.

Why This Book Will Help You

The Why Factor will help you because the principles are exceptionally simple to learn from and are easy to apply to your life. Instead of complex thought processes, the Why Factor relies on some very basic principles which already exist within us. For this reason, following the Why Factor can be a rather straight forward process. Beyond the advice listed in this book, it takes a bit of discipline to constantly question yourself as well as your surroundings. For this reason, the hardest work you need to complete within the Why Factor can be found within you.

This book will help you because you are ready to be helped. As we discussed, by reading this very sentence, you are a member of a very special group of people.

You are among the people who are asking themselves the question, "Why, Why Not Me?" Not only are you asking yourself this question, you are acting on the question. Since you are self-motivating and ready for change, this book is perfect for you. In time, you will see these positive results in more ways than one. You will see positive results professionally, personally and internally.

The Why Factor will help you identify which group you fall into as well as give you an action plan to fulfil your goals and aspirations. In a sense, The Why Factor will help you when it comes to starting your journey to success and if you are already successful, it will enhance your success. This book will teach you to always ask the question, "Why, Why Not Me". Not only will you learn to constantly ask yourself this question, you will learn how to act on your desires, dreams and goals. Remember when you were a child, or, if you have children, how often kids ask the question, "Why?" Children are always asking the question "Why? Why? Why? Why? Why?" They do it obsessively; they drill it down to find the core answer. This constant question, while simple, is one of the greatest ways children learn and grow. When we become adults, we stop asking the "Why? Why? Why? Why?" question. Within the Why Factor Academy, you will be re-introduced to this question many, many times.

So far, we have covered some very basic yet powerful principles to lead a healthy, positive and successful life. In time, you will learn to master the techniques in this book, and you will learn to apply these to your everyday life. Not just in the short term, but you will learn to apply the Why Factor to the rest of your life. Remember, the **Why Factor is a long term investment in your own personal growth and success.** Through this constant questioning, you will learn to build a positive and successful life source. **In medicine they say proper diagnosis of the problem is 50% of the cure.** By asking ourselves and using the "Why?" question we can drill down to the problem, the challenge, and begin to look and find the right answers and solutions to act upon.

The Three Aspects of a Successful Life

Some people are more successful than others because they are constantly looking to improve themselves through three key areas:

1. **Your Family & Personal Life-This is the Why? Your purpose in life**

2. **Your Personal Development-Personal self-development. Developing success habits**

3. **Your Career**

Many times, I will get to a roadblock in life and business and I ask myself, "Why the roadblock? There must be a way through this conflict. I must find a detour to get back on track in terms of living a successful life." For instance, think about driving through a town and needing to cross a river to get to the other side of town. Even if the bridges in town have been blown up or closed for construction, you need to find a way to get across the river. Remember, there is always a path to cross the river; you just need to work hard to find the best route to cross the river.

I believe that God has given us everything we need to be successful, but He is not going to do it for you, you have to do your bit. However, in order to succeed mentally and spirituality, we need to learn to control our mind. This can be an inner battle, or conflict within ourselves. However, modern society does not teach us to think this way. In school and in society, we are taught differently. We are taught to be the best in school, to have the biggest and best, but not necessarily what is best for us. We are taught that success is measured by being Number 1 or by having the biggest or fastest car. We are taught that success is having the largest house, or most expensively tailored suit. Remember, success in life is not only measured by material things or by whoever has the biggest and best toys etc. **What we have materially is a by-product of our skills and abilities to get results and the value we bring to the market.** It's about who finds the most happiness with their surroundings and circumstances.

Successful people understand that roadblocks or traffic jams in life or business are just a normal part of life. Everyone reaches roadblocks, traffic jams or setbacks in life; it's how we manage to navigate these challenging times that is important. Successful people do not allow roadblocks to get in their way in terms of long term success. Instead, they learn to overpower the roadblock through hard work, discipline and confidence. I love the quote from Lou Holtz, one of the premier American football coaches of our time, **"Life is 10% what happens and 90% of how you respond to it."** If you get this, you get the fact that you either take control of your situation or challenge or you give it away. Which one are you? Overcoming roadblocks is not easy, but there are a couple simple steps you can follow in order to reach a high degree of success.

1. You have to accept where you are today as a beginning and not an end

This is a big paradigm change; your mind needs to be open for new possibilities and new ways to move forward. Most people are in a state of denial in terms of where they are today, as well as the actual level of success they have achieved in life. In other words, they think they are a lot better off than they really are. For this reason, they can never move beyond the roadblocks of failure. Instead, they just stay at the roadblock, content with their current position in life. They act as though reaching the roadblock was the top of their successful story. They begin to develop a false sense of success and happiness. For this reason, you need to constantly ask yourself if you are at a roadblock in your life, and what actions you need to take to move beyond the roadblock.

Instead of accepting where you are today, you need to be honest with yourself. You need to accept the fact that you have reached a roadblock, and there exists a path to move beyond the roadblock. The roadblock is not the end of your journey. Remember, **you need to accept the fact that where you are today is a beginning of a starting point, and not the end point.** Once you can make this change your mind opens to new possibilities and new ways to move forward.

2. You need to research yourself and your past

I Remember Anthony Robins saying **"learn from the past but don't live in the past."** Another important part of finding a great path to success is to be honest with yourself. This involves researching yourself; where you have been in life and what events have shaped your current world, thinking and beliefs. This involves studying your past. For instance, a few important questions you need to ask yourself include, **"What should I have done differently?"**, **"What mistakes have I made?** and most importantly, **"Where has the current thought pattern in my life come from?" "What are my beliefs and where have those beliefs come from?"** "Are these beliefs that will make me successful or hold me back?"

Remember the law of cause and effect. **For every effect we experience there is a cause. If you can find the cause you can change the effect. By asking the Why question, you can find the cause.** You need to identify what the problem is in your life, both current and in the past and what caused it. For instance, think about the physical condition of high cholesterol. First, you need to accept the fact that you have high cholesterol, and next, you need to figure out what caused the high cholesterol. Many times, you might have consumed too many fatty foods like chips, burgers or steaks. Finally, you need to accept responsibility for the fact you have high cholesterol. You cannot blame others for your negative health, because when you blame others, you pass your power away and lose control of your life. Once you learn to accept responsibility, you can make the positive changes in your life needed to reduce your cholesterol.

Brian Tracy says, "When you blame, you live in the past and when you accept responsibility you look to the future."

People confuse accepting responsibility with guilt and blame. Most people do not want to accept responsibility because they think it means "it's my fault". **All the champions, leaders and successful people accept responsibility for their failures and successes.** They acknowledge their mistake, learn from their mistake, and move on. By learning from their own personal mistakes, they find a way to take the proper corrective actions, making sure to not make the same mistake again. Successful people understand this concept very well. They are keen to learn from their mistakes, and excited to grow from such mistakes. You see people who don't want to change anything but expect their life to be different...Hello? It is not going to happen to you.

CHAPTER 3

THE BIRTH OF THE WHY FACTOR

The Bakery

To share my own journey to building a happy and successful life, we turn to when I was a young man, aged twenty four. I was working in the music business with my Brother, Dele and we were going to be successful in the music business. However, it was the total opposite, nothing worked out and we lost the little money we had. I had hired a car, and took it back on an empty tank of fuel. When I returned the car to the car hire firm, they gave me my £5 deposit which I had left for the keys if I ever lost them. I remember standing in the road after turning in my car, saying to myself, "This is all I have... £5 to my name?" It was a rather low day for me. From here, I ended up sleeping on my friend Ellen's couch, and had to start over again. This failure led me to a hard job as a casual labourer, working in a bread factory.

Getting this job did not come easy. I had to stand in line outside the bakery with the other potential workers every day, hoping to get a day's work when demand was high. A truly humbling experience. I was never selected at first, but I kept coming back to the bakery door every day. Eventually, I was picked by the foreman to work for the day. I worked very hard that day, and was asked to come back the next day. I worked even harder the second day I was chosen, and continued to work harder and harder every day I was selected, simply because I was willing to work hard and willing to learn. Eventually, the Union workers became angry because the Manager was giving me all of the overtime hours. With redundancies at the bakery on the horizon, I needed to move on. I knew I could not continue to live with this sort of uncertainty as well as the low wage which came with the job. I desperately needed to make a change in my life. In many ways, the seed needed to change into a successful lifestyle was now planted in my head. So you can see I was a wanderer and, when the redundancy pattern interrupted my life, it caused me to ask, "Why am I in this position?"

In the beginning, I didn't have the money to take the bus to the bakery, so I would have to walk four miles, each way, and every day. I walked at night to the bakery, getting there about 9pm to start my shift at 10pm. In time, when I started catching up with my finances, I began to take the bus. Not the entire way. Instead, I would continue to walk part of the journey so I could save 24 pence on the bus fare. During these walks, I would see people pass me in luxury cars, driving BMWs, Jaguars and Mercedes. It was here that I started asking myself the question, "Why, Why Not Me?" "Why am I not one of the people driving a Mercedes or a Jaguar around town?" "What am I doing wrong, and where did it all begin to go wrong?" The "Why, Why Not Me" questions were beginning to ferment in my head.

WHY AM I NOT ONE OF THE PEOPLE DRIVING A MERCEDES OR JAGUAR, WHY NOT ME?

With the extra money I saved by walking a bit, as well as the extra income which came with the extra shifts at the bakery when possible, I found other ways to save money. For instance, at the bakery, we were allowed to eat as much bread as we wanted. So, I would bring a bit of butter to work and feast on a simple lunch of freshly baked bread and standard butter. This added to my savings, which allowed me to get off my friend's couch and into my own apartment once again. In many ways, I was back on the path to success. Whilst being a difficult and humbling period of my life, my experiences in the bakery helped me to begin my path to a successful and sustainable life.

During my time at the bakery, I asked myself: "Is this what God wanted or intended for me?" "Why am I not driving a Jaguar, Mercedes or BMW to work?" "Why not me?" "What do these people have that I do not have?" I finally reached the point in life where I was sick and tired of being sick and tired and something within me started asking the question, "Why, Why Not Me?" I am willing to learn, work hard and do whatever it takes so long as it's ethical and honest.

So, I began my path to get out of that situation, and never looked back. In a sense, I entered the Why Factor, and continued to keep this simple yet powerful style of thought in my head at all times. I looked at my options; I had no qualifications so I had a choice. I could go back to college, which was not an option, or go back to working in a factory, labouring, or find someone in a business that would train me. I already knew that direct sales were one of the few professions that takes people from all backgrounds and trains them. I answered an advert and got a job in Direct Sales. This position offered me the opportunity for tremendous growth and personal development. From those humble beginnings, I built a very successful business that ended up turning over 40 million pounds before I semi-retired. I was then Head Hunted to start a new business in the UK from scratch. Now, the business I run today does around 1 million pounds of sales per week in the UK alone and is one of the fastest growing regions worldwide. As you can imagine, my life is very different now than it was during the bakery days.

I tell you this story not simply to impress you but to impress upon you that anybody can do it if you are prepared to do the things successful people do. Success is something that can be learnt and achieved, it is not a gift. Once you start believing in yourself... "Why not you?" Can you give me one reason why you shouldn't be successful?

My Background

There are many parts to my story, as there are many parts to anyone's story. But to give you a proper perspective in terms of my background and upbringing, I think it's a good idea to start with experiences in school. In school, I like to say that I became a member of the Escape Committee, the group of students who escaped school as soon as it was legally allowed. While in school, my name was on the piece of paper, meaning, I was physically present, but my mind was always drifting out into the school yard and beyond. I did not learn like others, and it certainly took me longer to understand and comprehend concepts such as science and mathematics, I was regularly at the bottom of the class. For this reason, I sort of learned to shut school out of my mind, escaping from the system as soon as it was legally allowed. The sad part is that when I left college, I thought I wasn't clever and no good because that's what the education system sometimes does to people who do not excel. This reset point was critical. I was brought up, educated by the system or society, whichever you want to use, to believe that other people were better than me... can you relate to that? It would have been good if I had been brought up to ask, "Why were they better than me?" My talents were elsewhere, it just took a while to realise where these talents lay. That's why I believe that no matter where you are, what your past is, I believe you can change and improve your life and future using the Why Not Me? factor.

During the bakery experience, I was forced to confront what I was good at and what I was bad at. I knew I would never be the person who designed computer software, but that did not mean I could not succeed in business and in life. I thank my Mother and Father for their positive upbringing in business and in life. I was a shy person and knew I had to change and also, if I wanted to succeed, I had to learn to become a great communicator and develop great people skills. I began to realise my intellectual abilities related to how you speak to people, how to make deals happen, how to build value and so on. During the bakery experience, I realised I had to utilise my God-given talents in order to succeed in life, both professionally and personally.

Direct Sales is one of the few businesses which will allow you in without previous experience. It's an environment where you grow and develop. Then, you go onto the next challenge, which allows you to grow and develop even more. It's like climbing a ladder; each run represents a milestone of personal growth and happiness. Joining the world of sales, while constantly asking myself the question "Why" has given me a tremendous amount of professional and personal success.

CLIMB THE LADDER OF SUCCESS
ONE STEP AT A TIME

This is the path I found and took, there are many paths to success, but you won't find them if you are not looking.

Successful people learn from life experiences. They learn on the job through research, using mentors and getting to know people. For this reason, school was not the best learning environment for me. After leaving school, it took nearly eight years to believe in myself and learn that my education needed to be self-styled and self-taught. Working in sales gave me the drive, direction and path to achieve substantial success. I learned to pay attention to the successes and failures of the people around me. I learned to ask questions from people who were very successful within the realm of sales. "Why were they more successful than me?" I asked them for help. In other words, I asked qualified salesmen for relevant advice and guidance. For this reason, I consider myself a constant student of the world at large. **When you are green you are growing, when you are ripe and know it all, you are rotten.**

In terms of my background, I must say it is a bit different than your average Brit. I was born in London, but my mother is from Germany and my father is from Nigeria. Soon after my birth, my parents brought me to Nigeria to be raised in my father's native Africa. I have light skin, so on many occasions in school in Africa, I was bullied and picked on because of this; that was then and it is different now as the world has moved on. When I was 18, we moved back to the UK, where I was considered black. I have to laugh when I look back, but at the time it was not funny dealing with prejudices from both sides. For many years, this bothered me. But eventually, I realised you just have to deal with it; **you can't let other people's opinions hold you back.** I learned I cannot blame others for my background, or how people treated me in Africa or London, I learned that I'm not a colour, I am a person. Instead, when I look back on these experiences, I realised they helped me grow tremendously in the end. These experiences gave me a very thick skin. They taught me to ignore those who treated me harshly, and embrace those who treated me fairly. I love the serenity prayer: *"God grant me the serenity to accept the things I cannot change, the courage to change the things I can and the wisdom to know the difference".* In many ways, this is the start of the Why Factor.

My parents were quite influential when it came to building my work ethic as well as my positive and inquisitive attitude. When younger, my mother, a great teacher, taught me some very powerful principles. She used to say, "If you are going to do a job, make sure you do it properly." She drilled this mentality into me. I was taught always to be hard working. This mentality helped me stay focused on doing a great job no matter what it was. If I started something, no matter how hard it was, I would finish it. I would not quit until I accomplished the goals of the job. My mother taught me to never quit. Another great lesson my mother, Edith Martha, taught me was to **be careful how you treat people on the way up because you meet the same people on the way back down.**

While I have discussed a bit of my background, it is a good idea to turn to where all of our backgrounds start. In time, I will share my story in greater detail. But for now, let's all go back to day one in our lives. Think about the day you were born. When you look at your birth certificate, it puts baby boy or girl as well as your name and your parent's names. That's it. I wish they would put on your birth certificate, a column that says you can be anything you want to be in life.

Birth Certificate

Name and Surname _____
Sex _____
Date of Birth _____
Place of Birth _____
You can be anything you want _____
to be in life

_____ Superintendant Registrar

In many ways, our life starts with a blank birth certificate, and we add to this certificate as we move through life. Remember, we cannot help where we are born or what social condition we are born into. However, we need to take responsibility for the background we create for ourselves. For instance, ten years from now, looking back on the decade which just passed, you will add this period to your life background. In a sense, it becomes a part of your living birth certificate. For this reason, I like to think of our backgrounds as a moving, dynamic concept affecting our futures. Your background is not just your past; your background represents your possible future if you do not change. In other words, if your background is holding you back and you don't change, then your future will be the same as your past. Remember to take responsibility for the background you have created.

Why I Share My Story and Outline for Success

Beyond helping yourself, it is important to help others. This is especially true as we become more successful in life. We should all feel the duty to help others achieve happiness and success in their lives. By doing this, we enrich ourselves and we enrich our surroundings and make the world a better place. In many ways, I decided to share my story, both the successes and failures, so that you may relate and hopefully have the success in your life that you desire. Look at it this way: if you have been in a train crash, survived and was still standing, would you go back and help others?

The Why Factor Academy is the system which helped me. For this reason, I think it can be very useful to you and your personal journey towards a successful and positive future. Through my experiences, successes and failures, you are sure to save time, money and frustration when it comes to your own positive journey. As you read this book, it is important to recognise the makings of success, both through the example provided, as well as through the examples which influenced me through my personal journey.

The Why Factor is not a system for immediate success. Instead, the Why Factor journey is a process of continuous improvement. You see, there is no upper limit of success in the Why Factor, you will always be striving to become more successful and having fun doing so. For this reason, the Why Factor is more of a dynamic way of living. The "Why?" question you ask yourself today will be very different when compared to the "Why?" questions you will ask yourself in ten years. For this reason, remember that improvement within the Why Factor is a continuous, life-long process and when you embrace it, it's a lot of fun. What I have found is the "Why?" question proves that you are special and can do what other successful people do, if you are prepared to follow this system and programme. In other words success is not a gift or luck, it is learnt.

Success is like climbing a mountain. The further up the mountain you can go, the further you can see. So when you start the Why Factor journey, you may be starting at the bottom of the mountain, or you can be half-way up the mountain asking yourself why some people are more successful than others. Once you understand the concept, you begin to change your journey of climbing the mountain to success. You start at point A on the mountain, then move onto point B up the mountain, then point C, and so on. Each time, you get higher up the mountain, you see more of the positive scenery. The clouds part and the sun shines. You can see this beautiful scenery of the surrounding mountains and valleys. It is a truly healthy and positive experience as you move upwards. It is easier and safer to climb to the top of the mountain, following the path that has been laid out for you, by someone who has previously done it and easier still if you have a guide to walk with you. The Why Factor Academy is a guide to leading you upwards along the right path.

WHO IS YOUR GUIDE TO SUCCESS?

Sometimes when climbing the mountain of success, you will eventually hit a roadblock. When this happens, it is important to recognise the problem and quickly work towards a solution. If not, you will never be able to climb higher up the mountain. Remember, when life wants to teach you a lesson, it won't let you go until you learn the lesson. If you don't learn from it, it brings you back to point A. It might take you five, ten or even twenty years, and if you don't get it, the lesson never lets you go.

Another way to think of the upward improvement process of the Why Factor is to consider the game, Snakes and Ladders. As you make your way towards the top, the snake comes around and takes you back to the bottom of the pile or beginning of the game. You see, life, in many ways, is similar to the game Snakes and Ladders. So, you need to reflect on the Why Factor often throughout the remainder of your life. Ask yourself, "Why am I not improving in a particular area of my life?" "What can I do to fix it?" Once you have conquered this single particular problem, and when you get to the next level of understanding, you might reach another roadblock or traffic jam. Thus, returning to the beginning of the lesson you have not mastered, or going back to the same circumstances you found yourself in five or ten years ago. Simply put, this is the journey of life. You need to constantly review yourself and your circumstances, especially when you reach a roadblock.

I decided to share my story and outline for success, because it has been a very powerful tool for me, as well as the people I interact with on a daily basis. The Why Factor has helped members of my family, and it has helped many members of my business team. Through my experiences, I have trained many people and created an outline for success, which you can apply to your own life. By helping you achieve an added level of happiness and success, I am truly living to the principles of the Why Factor. This is the most important reason for sharing my system of success. Helping others to help themselves. I love the saying, **"feed a man a fish, feed him for a day. Teach him how to fish and you feed him for life."**

I hate it when I see people write other people off and say that they are no good, etc. We need to stop and look at their life, upbringing and challenges, in so far as people are so special with a unique DNA. Just because you may have been dealt a bad hand in life doesn't mean that you cannot turn your life around and win in the game of life. **You were born to succeed.** The only way to succeed is that you must want to learn and change.

Applying the Why Factor to your Every Day Life

While you can read the Why Factor in a week or two, it is important to remember this book is not a one-time read. Instead, it's a good idea to pick this book up every few months or so in order to re-evaluate your progress. By re-reading this book from time to time, you will be able to not only review your current surroundings and situations; you will retrain yourself to the terms and principles of the Why Factor. As you re-read this book, you might find one section more relevant than another section. You might find you missed an important point during your first read, only to understand such a fundamental concept of the Why Factor at a later date. This is a sign that you are growing.

This sort of dynamic learning experience is a great tool for long term success. In fact, it's the way the Why Factor was meant to work. As you read the book from time to time, your understanding of the principles will change. In many ways, you will reach a point on the mountaintop where you can see life from a completely different perspective. This, in turn, will change your understanding and interpretation of the Why Factor Academy. You see, the Why Factor is a powerful, dynamic system, capable of helping people of drive and discipline (just like you), no matter what stage in life you might find yourself. When you start asking "Why?" questions, you begin to capture why we are successful and why we fail, and this then becomes a library of positive and negative references to guide you through life successfully. Once you understand the Why, you understand you're just as good as anyone else and they are just doing something you are not doing yet. Then your self-esteem and confidence will begin to increase.

To apply the Why Factor to your life, you need to have the discipline to ask yourself the question, "Why?" on a daily basis. Take time to reflect on the answers and learn from them. It is a good idea to take notes as you go through the Why Factor and write down your thoughts and ideas, and study these notes using the "Why?" question. Here, you might find your notes to be ridiculous, or you might find that your notes are completely relevant and useful to your everyday life. No matter what the context, situation or reason for writing these notes, make sure to always ask the question, "Why?" In time, you will barely recognize the person (you) who started the wonderful journey that is the Why Factor.

One great tip: You will have already noticed you are beginning to ask yourself some "Why?" questions mentally. Please get a pen and paper or use this book and just write them down, don't answer them, instead just write the "Why?" questions that are in your head down and deal with them when you have finished the book.

To give you a preview of the topics to come in this book, the following table will help tremendously. Throughout the Why Factor Academy, we will turn to this list often, in order to make sure you are correctly implementing a proper plan of success. In a sense, consider these ten steps to be the ingredients needed in order to make the best recipe for success:

Ten Steps to Success within the Why Factor Academy

1. Set Clear, Specific Goals

2. Believe in Yourself

3. Establish Your Quit Ability Point

4. What Skill Level Is Needed to Obtain Your Goal

5. Develop a Plan of Action

6. Work Ethic & Discipline

7. Building a Time Table for your
   Success

8. Accept Feedback

9. Accept Full Responsibility for the
   Outcome of Your Goals

10. Fast Tracking Success: Listen, Learn
    and Apply

CHAPTER 4

THE WHY? WHY ME? PEOPLE

To start the process of learning the ins and outs of the Why Factor Academy, we start with understanding the "Why, Why Me?" question. In other words, we need to understand who the "Why Me?" people are, and why they are the way they are. If you currently find yourself as the "Why, Why Me?" type of person, then ask yourself, "Why are you like that?" "Why do you feel sorry for yourself?" etc. Use the Why Factor to break loose. In time, you can certainly master the skills to become a great candidate for the Why Factor Academy. Remember, I was once a "Why, Why Me?" person. So, living within the "Why, Why Me?" mentality is not the end of the road for you by any means.

The purpose of this chapter is **not** to disregard or degrade a large group of society. Instead, it is important for you to identify which group you belong to so you can take the necessary action to move forward. By learning from the failures and successes of others, we find a way to avoid similar flaws and traps, or success habits to copy. The more you understand the four groups, the easier it becomes for you to control yourself, before you slip back into the wrong group. It helps you identify, as you talk with people, what group they are in and how to identify them. To help you identify the traits of a "Why Me?" person, we turn to a few examples.

Examples of the Why Me People

Why am I always unlucky?

Why do all these have to happen to me?

Why am I always ill?

Why don't I drive the car I want to drive?

Why do I always end up with the wrong partner?

Why do I have to go and do a job I hate?

Why did I get fired or made redundant?

Why me? It's not fair

Why did I get divorced?

Why do I never get my own way?

Why am I the Princess of the Pity Party?

Why do I never have any money?

Why am I not good enough?

Why don't I have many friends?

WHY ME? WHY DO I NEVER HAVE ENOUGH MONEY? ITS NOT FAIR.

This simple list includes a few common traits of the "Why, Why Me?" type of person. You see, instead of acting to resolve their problems, they feel sorry for themselves and can never seem to dig their way out of the problem. These tend to be the people who see the glass as being half empty. For this reason, when entering the Why Factor Academy, you need to be aware of these traits and make sure you abandon the things in your life which cause you to ask such questions. We will show you how to deal with this if you want to change. Remember, within this book, we will show you how to handle these sort of questions and show you how the active "Why, Why Not Me?" people are the ones who refuse to live with their misery, and how you can become one of them. Remember, misery is one of the unfortunate traits of the "Why, Why Me?" mentality. If one of your goals in life is to be happy, then being a "Why, Why Me?" professional will never achieve that.

First, let's consider a close friend of mine, a carpenter who, to protect his identity, we will call Barmy. Barmy is a great person and a hard worker, but he is definitely a "Why, Why Me?" person. He is great at what he does, but he hates his job. So why is this? How can Barmy hate his job, but love his work? For one, Barmy should have taken the steps needed to open his own carpentry business. Instead, he has to work for a boss who doesn't treat him with dignity and respect, who makes him work nights and weekends. Not only does this make Barmy a bit cranky at work, it has made him a bit cranky at home sometimes. If Barmy had taken the correct steps in order to start his own business, or change jobs and find a better boss, and by doing so, building his own destiny, Barmy would be a very different person. But Barmy chose not to take the actions needed in order to improve his life. He is still asking himself the "Why Me?" question instead of the active "Why, Why Not Me?" answer. I hope he makes the transition to the "Why Not Me?" sort of mentality soon. You see the "Why, Why Me?" mentality locks you into the problem and the circumstances, because you are constantly accepting where you are as a state.

Another type of "Why, Why Me?" person, which often cracks me up, is when the "Why, Why Me?" person says, "I should have known better". But if they knew better, they would not have made the mistake in the first place! Sometimes we know better and don't act. "Why didn't we act?" That's the real answer and where the problem and solution is. So, you can't use this expression in the Why Factor Academy. Instead, when living in the Why Factor, **you need to accept responsibility for your actions and acknowledge your mistakes.** Catching yourself and doing something about it is the key to reprogramming your thinking and this is the beginning of change.

In life, there are mistakes which are harder to recover from. However, it can be done. The vast number of issues we face on a daily basis, we can recover from without much effort. Sometimes, the large obstacles we see are actually small pebbles, when compared to the stories of others. Let's say, for instance, you had to declare bankruptcy. However, there are lots of stories of successful people who, at least once in their lifetime, had to declare bankruptcy. Instead of giving up, they built their fortune back. I like to use Donald Trump as an example. While he is now a globally known billionaire, his life was once very different. While he grew up in Forest Hills Gardens and was raised in a family with money, his fortunes once reached the point of bankruptcy. He took a risk which did not work out.

What separates Donald Trump from others is the fact he refused to give up. Donald Trump did not become a "Why, Why Me?"

person. Instead, he was smart enough and worked hard enough to remain a "Why, Why Not Me?" person. At his darkest hour, Donald Trump was walking home and saw a beggar on the street with a few cents in his can. He turned to his wife and said, "You see that man, he is richer than we are right now." But he came back, learned from his mistakes and is now one of the most successful people on the planet. Remember, he lost everything, but he built his empire again. And so can you. The only time you fail is when you quit. I will say that again. The only time you fail in life is when you quit. **Quitters never win and winners never quit.**

Let me ask you a question, "Are you a quitter?" Interesting question isn't it?

Donald Trump is one of thousands and thousands of successful people in the country in the world. Who, when they are faced with adversity, did not quit and went on to be successful. You too are as good as any one of them, if you rise to the challenge.

The "Why, Why Me?" sort of person does not have the ability or motivation to move onto greater success like Donald Trump, as discussed, the pessimism holds them back. You need to make sure you can navigate your challenges correctly instead of caving in to short term pressures. In essence, you just need to make sure you do not turn into a "Why, Why Me?" person along the way. Remember, even if all the bridges in town are destroyed or closed for construction, you need to find a path to get to the other side of town. It takes work, brains, asking "Why?" questions, directions, and so on. You need to remember that a solution to your travel problems does exist. You just need to find the solution and have the discipline to see the solution through.

Negatives of the Why? Why Me? Mentality

As you can imagine by this point in the chapter, there are many negatives which come with the "Why, Why Me?" mentality. In a sense, the "Why, Why Me?" people tend to get stuck in a rut, and do not know how to navigate out of the problem. In time, the problem only gets worse and worse. It's sort of like being on an endless rollercoaster, moving from high to low. However, even when it feels as if you have made a bit of progress, when you view the problem in its entirety, you will notice that the problem has not truly changed. Your worries have not lessened at all. Instead, your negative attitude has reclaimed you into a sense of acceptance. You are now an official pessimist. The worry cycle. You worry then you think about what could go wrong, then you analyze how bad it could get and then you worry some more and repeat the cycle again and again and again until it paralyses you mentally from taking action.

The negatives of the "Why, Why Me?" mentality are best seen from the long term point of view. On the day you accept the "Why, Why Me?" mentality, life might not seem that bad. However, as you continue to enforce this mentality year after year, decade after decade, the problem becomes worse in time. The mounting problems might not seem noticeable, but they have certainly become worse with time. So, in time, the negatives tend to compound.

Think about our example of the mountain, but imagine the mountain covered in snow. The "Why, Why Me?" person will probably quit and not make it to the top. If they reach their highest level on the mountain, then they start to fall downwards. In time, they pick up speed and a lot of dirt. When the "Why, Why Me?" person finally reaches the bottom, their lives tend to shatter into pieces. For this reason, the longer you spend in the "Why, Why Me?" phase of your life, the greater the risks. It is truly unfortunate to see people reach this point in their lives, but it is also important to recognize that this sort of scenario happens to a lot of people in this world. I too was a victim, I just fought back. For this reason, you need to be wary of the negatives of the "Why, Why Me?" mentality, especially as time passes.

Finally, one of the negatives of the "Why, Why Me?" mentality is the fact that some people actually revel in their own misery. They have grown accustomed to the "Why, Why Me?" way of life. The miserable "Why, Why Me?" people are not just happy to own their own misery; they want to bring other people into their miserable worlds to share in their misery. For this reason, it is important to avoid the "Why, Why Me?" miserable people whenever possible. Beyond this, you need to remain aware of your own personal relationships with the outside world. For instance, you need to make sure you do not share your pessimism with the world, and you do not blame the world for your pessimism. **Pessimism, in every form, has no place in the Why Factor Academy.**

The people you associate with and talk to every day will influence your success. Stop and think about the statement you have just read. If you hang around a "Why Me?" pessimistic type of person, it will make your success in life a lot harder. My Mother used to always say to me, "**If you hang around with dogs you will get fleas.**"

Depressed, Stressed and Anxious

Some of the qualities commonly associated with the "Why, Why Me?" people include stress, depression and anxiety. If you are stressed and depressed, it's because you have lost control of your surroundings and situations but most importantly your thoughts (thinking). You have relinquished control and given someone else power over your happiness; you believe you have no control or influence over your life. If you are stuck in a rut, it's because you keep telling yourself you are stuck in a rut. You feel good about yourself to the degree of control you have in your life. **When you are in control of your life, you are happy; when you lose control you are unhappy.**

If you feel unhappy right now, ask yourself, when have you lost control? Why? Make a note and we can deal with it later.

Why have you lost control?

In life, we tend to get wrapped up in circumstances and situations which affect our confidence, causing us to take on the "Why, Why Me?" mentality. So, when this happens, we tend to accept our current lives and surroundings. A startling statistic I heard recalls the fact that over 70 % of people hate their jobs (Forbes). But why? For one, they are only working in their current jobs because it pays the bills. But the question they need to be asking themselves is much simpler: Why not find a job which makes you happy and which can also pay the bills?

It's sort of like my friend Barmy, who is always saying, "I hate my job". So one day, I asked him, "then why don't you find another job?" But six months later, he was still working in the same job. Not only was he working in the same job, he was hating the same job. Deep down, I know Barmy wants to do something with his life. Instead, Barmy has chosen not to act on his true abilities. Instead, he has chosen to live behind a mask of denial. Some people have caved in and thrown in the towel.

To alleviate the symptoms of stress, depression and anxiety, we need to acknowledge the source of the stress, depression and anxiety. Sometimes, the sources of our problems are related to our diets. You might be drinking too much caffeine, or beer, or smoking too much tobacco. You might eat too much fried and unhealthy food and shy away from the foods which are good for your body and mind. Eating the right foods plays a big part in your state of mind. Eating healthily nutritional foods, especially vegetables, will help you change your state of mind. For this reason, to avoid stress, depression and anxiety, it is important to start with your own health. If you feel sluggish, you will have a sluggish life. Once you have found a proper balance of nutrition and health, you can move onto solving the other problems in your life which are causing the stress, depression and anxiety. Sometimes, your living conditions might be the source of your problems. Other times, the problems might involve watching too much TV or spending too much time on the couch.

Beyond our diet and surroundings, to reduce stress, depression and anxiety, we sometimes need to cut ties with the people around us who are bad negative influences or are too much of a burden. You need to get rid of your other "Why, Why Me?" friends you associate with. While it can be hard to say goodbye to old relationships, at times, we need to realise when it is best to part ways with a bad influence. You would be surprised how easy it is to reduce stress, depression and anxiety when you eliminate bad influences from your life. Offer your pessimistic friends the Why Factor to change and see their reaction. Chances are they will give you an excuse. They actually are content with where they are.

Stress, depression and anxiety are toxic qualities and the reason for some of our health issues and in other words, '**dis-eases'** we have today. If you give into any of these traits, you can never leave the grasp of the "Why Me?" mentality. If you allow yourself to be surrounded by the toxic nature of stress, depression and anxiety, you are sure to take on these qualities, most of what we stress about never happens. Look at all the things you have worried about and how many actually happened. Don't get me wrong, but don't confuse being cautious and calculating the risk, with stress and worry.

Conscious versus Subconscious

When people live with the "Why Me?" mentality, they tend to get lost in a game between the conscious state and the subconscious state. For example, if you say to yourself that you are stupid, your subconscious will cause you to do stupid things. If you say I am not good at remembering names, immediately your subconscious state will erase any new names you encounter. This is very important: **if you do not control your thoughts then you don't control your actions and destiny.** "Why Me?" is a thought. Where did you get it from? You see we need to understand how the brain works; whatever conversation you are having in your conscious mind, whether you have thought about what you are saying or not, is predicting and controlling your present and future. Your conscious mind is the control tower that gives direct instructions to your subconscious, who is an obedient servant that will deliver.

Too often, the "Why, Why Me? people allow their subconscious to take control of their reality, work and surroundings without taking control of their conscious thoughts. In many ways, once you allow your conscious mind to give into the "Why, Why Me?" way of thinking; in other words believing in the "Why Me?" syndrome, your subconscious goes to work delivering the very things you are telling yourself. If you say to yourself, "I am not good at anything". Your subconscious says, "Don't worry, I'll take care of that for you," and makes sure you are not good at anything.

Since our thoughts ultimately control our actions, surroundings and circumstances, we need to learn to control our thoughts in a positive way. We all know that a bag of crisps is bad for you. However, some people eat crisps twice or more a day. This sort of behaviour is bad for your taste buds and mind, and in the end, it can send you to an early grave. We know this, but we decide to eat the bad food for one simple reason: it tastes really, really good. Our body, in this case, has taken over control of our minds. Therefore, we need to make sure we can control our mind, body and brain by asking the "Why?" questions. We can learn to be able to discipline ourselves to make the correct life choices required. "Why am I overweight?" You will probably have to ask the question 10-20 times before you get to the bottom of it. If you answer the question honestly, you will get to the solution. It is simple but not easy.

Secondly, we need to learn to listen to our bodies. Sometimes, this involves cooking and eating healthier foods, and other times the process of listening to our bodies includes matters related to exercise. Beyond the physical nature of our bodies, we need to remember to pay attention to the spiritual part of our minds. You cannot form happiness and success without a peace of mind. So peace and mind comes from your spiritual beliefs. As you can imagine, it is difficult to manage all these important traits. Attaining this balance does not come easy to many people, and the difficulty of maintaining this balance is the reason why some people remain within the "Why, Why Me?" mentality. However, the first step is to identify the areas that you need to work on and then start. It doesn't matter where you start. It's like tidying a room or a drawer, it doesn't matter where you start, just start tidying.

Losing Control of Your Life

For the "Why, Why Me?" people, it is very easy for them to lose control of their lives. As we discussed, some people take a long time to reach rock bottom, and other people can reach this point rather quickly and often. For this reason, it is important to recognize that some people unconsciously sabotage their own success. You cannot help an alcoholic until they accept they drink too much and need help. The same with weight. You cannot lose weight until you accept that you are too heavy, you can't accept your problem until you understand why you have it. For example, "Why am I overweight?" Asking the "Why?" question is one of the most powerful questions you can ask yourself. So, coming to terms with reality is the most important part of the Why Factor Academy. **This is your starting point for success.**

There are many reasons why people lose control. Sometimes, a person will lose control of their lives after a divorce or passing of a close loved one. These life changing events can certainly cause someone to lose control of their surroundings. However, we must always remember that there is an acceptable time of bereavement, that life moves on, and so must we. Again the serenity prayer is one I use all the time: accept what you cannot change and change the things you can. You can change. How do I know all this? Because I was once that "Why, Why Me?" person with issues, excuses and the Why Factor taught me how to fight for my life. Asking "Why? Why Not Me?" instead, helped me remain positive and in control at all times. Remember, the Why Factor Academy needs you to remain positive and in control at all times. You need to always remain an optimist.

While this chapter might have seemed a bit deep, it is important to remember that we only discussed the "Why, Why Me?" people in order to understand how we can get caught up in the trials and tribulations of the "Why, Why Me?" mentality. In other words, by understanding the characteristics of the "Why, Why Me" people, we can learn how to avoid these lifestyle choices and then change our futures. Understanding why you are a "Why Me?" person can help you become a "Why Not Me?" You were born to succeed, don't ever forget that. Yes to succeed!!

The Law of Accident

This is the last topic we are going to cover with reference to the "Why? Why Me?" people. A law I see practiced frequently is best described as the **Law of Accident**. The Law of Accident means you give up control and responsibility of your life and success. People who live by this law just live life by accident. Everything that happens to you happens by luck, by accident, by chance and not by design. It's like driving a car with no steering wheel. In many ways, people who live by the Law of Accident accept what comes to them, both positive and negative. Their attitude is only as good as the last thing that happened to them. For this reason, you need to make sure you do not live by the Law of Accident.

If you are a "Why? Why Me?" person, you need to keep asking yourself "Why?" "Why?" And drill down to find what happened, what circumstances or events caused you to see yourself as not worthy, not good enough. Some of the answers you are looking for can be found in your childhood. "Why?" Once you understand what happened, then you can begin the journey to a more self-fulfilled life.

Closing this section, the Why Factor is a program to help you move from where you are today to where you want to be tomorrow. If you are a "Why Me?" person, you don't have to live in that world anymore, you can change. The process of change is to accept that there is a problem. Second step is to ask "Why?" you have the problem, so that you can establish the root of the problem. The third step is to establish a plan with the fourth step being to execute the plan. It sounds simple but it's not, it's going to take time as there is more to learn, it is important to finish the book first before you judge it. If you tried to eat a half-baked cake, you wouldn't enjoy it as much as a fully baked cake, so finish the book.

Ask yourself: "Am I ready to change today and become the person I was born to be?" The Why Factor will help you on that journey.

AM I READY TO START CHANGING TODAY AND BECOME THE PERSON I WAS BORN TO BE?

As I reflect back, there were many times in my earlier life where I would, after setbacks and failures, say "Why, Why Me?" Fortunately I learnt to go from asking "Why Me?" to "Why Not Me?" That changed my paradigm. If you are reading the Why Factor today, I challenge you to ask yourself, "Why Not You? Why Not You?" Then pause and listen to yourself, listen to the dialogue in your brain, that's where the blockage is.

Why not you?

Start believing you are special and born successful in many ways...**let's take the journey together and discover the unbelievable potential you have...**

CHAPTER 5

"WHY, WHY NOT ME?"

Remember, there are two types of "Why, Why Not Me" people. One group of people have the talent and ability to improve their lives, but fail to act on their abilities. Putting it honestly, they "talk the talk, but don't walk the talk." They are the passive "Why? Why Not Me" people. The other group of "Why, Why Not Me" active people, are the people who have the talents to improve and take corrective actions in order to become more successful; again putting it honestly, **they talk the talk and walk the talk**, they are the active "Why? Why Not Me" people. This is the segment of society who are constantly improving themselves as well as their surroundings. They challenge themselves daily with the belief that they can be better, stronger and more disciplined and are continually improving their skills and successes. The "Why? Why Not Me?" active group are the group that produce all the successful people and our goal in the Why Factor Academy is to move you from any group into the "Why, Why Not Me?" active group, so you can begin to enjoy the successes you were born to achieve. Instead of being satisfied with your current or past state, you are the type who are actively making and seeking positive changes in your life. Since you have taken actions in the past, and working towards a more proper review of your life, you are certainly the active "Why, Why Not Me?" sort of person and are on the road to success. As you know, the "Why, Why Not Me?" type of person realises that there is always room for improvement in ones' life.

In this chapter, we will discuss the "Why, Why Not Me?" type of mentality. Beyond the simple descriptors of the "Why, Why

Not Me?" sort of person, we will discuss some examples of "Why, Why Not Me?" people. We will also discuss a group of people who are close to being "Why Not Me? people, but lack the motivation to make substantial changes in their lives. As you read this chapter, make sure to identify which qualities are easy for you to adapt to your life, as well as the qualities which might take some time to add to your daily routine.

The "Why, Why Not Me?" type of people can be a complex group of people. In other words, there is no set path to living a successful life. Also, there is not one single style of success. Instead, **you need to determine what type of success you want to achieve in life and what success means to you.** This is very important, in order to then develop a plan to achieve this success. It is important to learn from the success and failures of "Why, Why Not Me?" active people. You see, the one quality which all active "Why, Why Not Me?" people share is the quality of never giving up. They take calculated risks, they enjoy their success and they learn from their failures. The active "Why, Why Not Me?" people are the people who work hard and live positive lives; these are optimists in all situations. In time, you will learn the ins and outs of becoming an active "Why, Why Not Me?" person.

First Category - Optimists with no action game plan (Type B)

When we speak about the "Why, Why Not Me?" type of person, there are two types of people. One group of people that, because they have the ability, believe that they don't need to act on their desires; while the second group believes they have the ability and do take action on it. It's sad to see people who have the ability to achieve greatness and they never act on their talents or abilities. For this reason, it is a good idea to spend a bit of time discussing how and why these two groups of people are slightly different.

When I speak to people who have been unsuccessful at times, they tend to explain how close they were to becoming successful, only to watch the success drift away. They climb the mountain and reach a cliff and plunge over the side of the cliff. This happens to a lot of people, the successful ones get up and go again and the unsuccessful ones give up on their aspirations, sort of telling themselves to walk away. They see themselves that they gave it their best, they throw the towel in and give up, instead of dusting themselves off and trying again. They allow the event to scar them mentally. At this point you have accepted your mistake/error as failure and realised it is not for you. This is known as learned hopelessness. Remember the story I told you earlier about the baby elephant and its conditioning... this is how we get conditioned as human beings and a lot of this happens in our childhood.

The "Why, Why Not Me?" passive person has a big ego, they believe the world owes them and not they owe the world, they do not have the drive to act on their path to success, which is one of the greatest differences between the two types of "Why, Why Not

Me?" people: one is passive, the other is active. Make sure to constantly act on the things you are passionate about. Beyond acting on your passions, you always need to remember to never give up. Once you give up, you have psychologically accepted that you have given it your best, this is it, and you can't win. This psychological scar will hold you back in life unless you keep on saying, **"Why Not Me?" "I can do this, I can win!"** Remember the story of the Elephant, if you have all the qualities of a "Why, Why Not Me?" person, but lack the motivation to learn or change, you are not a "Why, Why Not Me?" person, you are a wanderer in disguise.

Second Category - Optimists with a game plan (Type A)

There are many ways to describe and categorize the "Why, Why Not Me?" active sort of mentality. Firstly, the "Why, Why Not Me?" Active person always makes sure to question themselves on a daily basis. The "Why, Why Not Me?" people are very active when it comes to constantly improving themselves and their surroundings. "Why, Why Not Me" people are positive, always learning from failures instead of sulking on the occasional or constant defeat.

Secondly, when the "Why, Why Not Me?" active person reflects on the world, they see that life is simply an evolving process. It's a constant evolution with lots of ups, downs and surprises. **Life is like a roller coaster ride, once you are strapped in that's it.** There are scary bits, boring bits, fun bits you just have to hold on and enjoy the ride but you don't quit half way. However, the "Why, Why Not Me?" people are never quite satisfied with their status and surroundings. Instead, the "Why, Why Not Me?" people want to constantly change for the better. They fear going to the grave, with their sweetest music as yet unheard. They fear living an unfulfilled life, for ten, twenty, thirty or forty/fifty plus years.

With this said, the "Why, Why Not Me?" type of person needs to focus on three distinct areas of their life to bring real improvement. These three key areas are:

1. **Your Career**

2. **Your Personal Family**

3. **Your Personal Development**

Your Career

The "Why, Why Not Me?" person makes sure to focus a large amount of attention on their career. A fulfilling career gives you satisfaction, confidence, a feel good factor about yourself - and obviously money. Now money isn't everything and money can't buy you happiness, but I would rather be rich and miserable than poor and miserable, and believe me, I have tried both. Money brings comfort and stability, and we all need to use money on a daily basis. We live in a world today where it is really hard to survive without it. As we progress in our careers, we tend to make more money. Truly successful people know how to bring in multiple sources of revenue, giving them a considerable amount of financial stability. **Once you realise it takes the same amount of time to succeed as it does to fail,** for this reason, it is important to constantly question where you are in your career. **Will your current career or job deliver what you need financially; in order to do the things you would like to do and provide the lifestyle you want for you and your family?** If not, then ask the question, **"Why Not?"** Then, **"Why am I doing this job/following this career path?"**

There is nothing wrong in making good money if you have earned it honestly and ethically. Money is like alcohol; for some people it brings out the best and for others the worst.

Making a lot of money is definitely not the only factor in the Why Factor. Instead, we judge success in the Why Factor through **happiness, fulfilment and integrity, and your contribution to society in helping others.** Certainly, you can be a successful member of the Why Factor and be a bread maker, a Social Worker, Nurse, Doctor, Engineer, etc. Provided, of course, you are happy and content with your current circumstances. For this reason, it is very important to always remember **that money is not the key to success; happiness is the key to success.** This is especially true when it comes to choosing your career path.

When "Why, Why Not Me?" people consider their careers, they are much disciplined when it comes to correctly plotting the course of their career. Meaning, they research what it will take to achieve their goals. Sometimes, to reach a goal, a financial measure is needed. Think of a university education. Certainly, you need to consider the financial aspects of your schooling before you undertake such an important investment and **will the education get you the job you want?** It's sad to see a university graduate not being able to get a job in the qualification sector they studied and having to go back to university to get another degree; if only they had known this at the beginning. Other times, to achieve ones' career goals, you need to think about the concept of time. **You see, what we really do is exchange our working time for money and the money you make is directly related to the value you give to your company/business etc. and how easy it is to duplicate you.** Don't take this the wrong way, if you are paid £7 per hour, £10 per hour or even £100 per hour that is the value you bring to your company. So the more value you bring to your company or your business, the more money you make and the more successful you become. I see people asking for more money but they never first ask themselves if they are adding more value. How much time will you have to spend in an aeroplane before you can be considered a certified pilot? How many years will it take you to reach the corner office in your company? These are just two of many simple questions you will have to manage when considering your career path as a Why, Why Not Me person. Simply put there are 86,400 seconds in a day to spend, you have to spend it wisely, invest it wisely or it is gone forever. Imagine you had £86,400 to spend a day and you kept wasting it and not investing, you would still have nothing but memories. Reading the Why Factor and any other educational books, CD's, attending seminars, training programs, etc., is a wise investment of your time.

Your Personal Family

Besides your career, as a "Why, Why Not Me?" person, you need to focus on you and your personal family. If you only focus on your career, you are sure to have a miserable family. Instead, in the Why Factor, you need to recognise the role and happiness of your family in your own success. With this said, the way you focus on your family has nothing to do with how many cell phones or tablets you provide to your children. Focusing on your family involves listening to their spiritual, parental and health needs and giving them time. Some of those 86,400 seconds a day must be spent with them. You cannot spend all the time with your family and nothing in your career, there has to be a balance. Sometimes it will be out of balance and that's where a great partner comes in;

you can't do it without support. **It is also important for your family to understand what you do, and why you do what you do.** The more they understand, the better it is.

Learning to balance your work and family can be a difficult task to manage. You might have a position which requires long hours or intense travelling. Or, you might own your own small shop which requires your constant attention. For this reason, it can be difficult to balance your responsibilities at work and at home. During the course of your Why Factor training, it is important to examine how much time you are devoting to your family, and if this amount of time is appropriate. Alternatively, you need to make sure you are spending enough time earning money to provide for your family. For this reason, the balance of work to family can be quite complex. By learning the methods in this book, you will find it much easier to balance your work-family responsibilities. Looking back, I made some mistakes and yes, I should have done some things differently. Hopefully, I will be able to help you amend some of these as you go through the Why Factor.

Your Personal Development

This is another pillar of the "Why, Why Not Me?" type of person and probably one of the most important. Instead of working towards a promotion or a happier family, with Personal Development, you are focusing on your own improvement. Improving your character, personality, habits, people skills and, most importantly, how you think and process information. **Improve yourself, improve your life**. To earn more you have to learn more. Improving ourselves goes well beyond work and family. Instead, personal improvement includes our health, fitness, wellness and spirituality and most importantly, the way we think, analyze and process information. In order to help others, we need to be able to help ourselves. For this, cooking and eating correctly is an important part of personal development. It is not very hard to eat correctly, and as we age, we need to learn to eat differently to alleviate certain illnesses.

We need to look at the types of food we eat and how it is cooked. **Look at your plate and ask yourself, "What's this doing for my health and wellbeing?"**

"WHAT IS YOUR PLATE SAYING TO YOU?"

For this reason, nutrition and health are a very dynamic aspect of our personal development. There is so much information out there today to help you understand that good healthy food is natural medicines. Hippocrates said, **"Let thy food be thy medicine and thy medicine be thy food."** You need to realise what is going on in the inside and not what's going on the outside determines your health. We tend to focus and spend more on the outside, clothes, makeup and how we look, etc., and we don't focus on what we are putting inside our bodies.

You wouldn't put the wrong fuel into an Aston Martin, Bentley or Ferrari would you?

Within the Why Factor, personal development can be a very wide ranging subject to cover. Certainly, there are many people who find religion to be a great way to grow spiritually. Since we cannot cover every type of personal development, it is important to research which actions will add positively to your life. Remember, within the Why Factor, research is critical. Not just research, but you need to know how to find information from qualified sources.

Examples of "Why, Why Not Me?"

There are so many success stories of people who have changed their life course in many positive ways. As an example, let's consider Sir Richard Branson. He left school when he was 16 years of age and moved to London to start up a magazine called 'Students'. In many ways, Richard Branson was a fellow member of the Escape Committee. However, he is certainly not lazy and he is certainly not stupid. Instead, Richard Branson built a global brand with tremendous success and reach. At the start of his business career, Sir Richard had a vision and concept. He knew deep down inside that his vision would work and be successful, but he was not always able to convince people that his business model was so powerful. At first, people laughed at him, but they are no longer laughing. Instead, they wish they had listened. The important point here is you have to believe in yourself, why not you.

As another example, look at the progression of David Beckham. He progressed from being a talented youth player, to being a premier member of Manchester United and then Real Madrid. When he first joined the premier league, Eric Cantona was the top guy on the team at the time. What Beckham noticed was that Cantona spent an extra hour or two practicing on his skills, after everyone else had left for the day. To be the best, Beckham realised he had to work just as hard as Cantona. He started spending time with Cantona during these extra practice sessions. You see, the real success of David Beckham came from the amount of time he spent practicing his craft, the free kick.

I was told that during these practice sessions, Beckham would tie a car tyre to the goal post and try and hit the ball through the tyre. At first his success rate was poor, in time he got better and better and better. **With practice, perfection comes to all.** So when an extra kick was needed, Beckham was the man called all the time. He has an extraordinary work ethic and discipline behind the scenes. And this is the reason for his success; hard work and discipline.

Food for thought, when you see anyone successful it's important to realise how many hours they put into their skill to perfect it. We think it is talent, when in most cases its **belief, time, effort, commitment and**

discipline put into action. If you wanted to score yourself on:

Belief ☐

Time ☐

Effort ☐

Commitment ☐

Discipline ☐

What score would you give yourself out of 10?

Will Smith is another great example of a hardworking, disciplined, talented Why Not me type of person. Will once said on a TV interview, **"When people are sleeping, I am working. When people are eating, I am working".** This is the type of commitment you need to be great. Most of the time, people want success, but they are not willing to work for it. Have you heard the saying that **everyone wants to go to Heaven but nobody wants to die**? Now, we don't have to die to succeed, but we have to have commitment to the cause. However, as we can tell from our examples, the people who are successful want to and are willing to work for their success. They achieve their goals.

"Why, Why Not Me?" Are Positive People

One common quality of all "Why Not Me" people can be traced to their state of mind. "Why Not Me" people are all positive people, they are optimists. Instead of reflecting on what can or has gone wrong, they focus on what has or will go right. They do not take risks based on the chances of failure. Instead, **they take risks based on the chances of success.** Einstein had a quote, **"in the middle of every difficulty lies opportunities."**

IN THE MIDDLE OF EVERY DIFFICULTY LIES OPPORTUNITIES.

In order to live the life of a Why Factor student, you need to constantly remain an optimistic person. **There is no room for negativity in your life** when you follow this program, so it is important to quickly identify any negative or pessimistic thoughts you have before acting on them. With this said, you are sure to encounter a lot of experiences in your life where the negative answer is correct. If someone comes to you and tells you to invest £100 in a project, so that you can receive £10,000 in a month, you are best to walk away from the deal. In other words, you cannot simply wish positive things to come true in your life. Instead, you need to navigate the world, understanding where positive outlets exist and where negative caves can be found. In time, you will learn how to identify the positive and optimistic aspects of the world, as well as the negative and pessimistic tendencies of the world and people.

Steering Yourself towards a Successful Path

In order to steer yourself towards a successful career, family and personal life, there are few first steps you need to take. **Number One: You need to establish what you want to do with your life: What's your purpose in life? Number Two: You need to understand the commitment and price you need to pay in order to get it.** Without recognizing these two crucial elements of your path to success, you cannot determine the correct and true path to reach your success.

First, you need to determine what you want to do with your life and what your purpose in life is. Get a pen and paper, make time. In fact do it now if it is appropriate. This is serious stuff; this is your life we are talking about. Make time for your life. If you are 50 years old, you might not want to choose a career path which takes 10 years to achieve, so make sure to pick a realistic goal in terms of your current stage of life. Ask yourself what lifestyle you want for you and your family and why? What income do you want to earn a month and why? What do you enjoy doing and why? Can you make a career out of it or is it a hobby? Do you want to be your own boss? Why? The clearer you can establish what you want out of life, the quicker and simpler it is to achieve, so please take the time to figure out what you want.

Secondly, you need to understand the cost of achieving your goals. **Nothing in life is free**, and achieving your goals is just another example of this common saying. Instead, achieving your goals takes more than money. It takes time, commitment, experience, hardship, discipline, etc. So, before you get too far into your desired career, you need to establish how hard you are willing to work to achieve your goals. In other words, you need to establish a **Quit Ability Point**. Here, you will establish just how far you are prepared to go to achieve your goals. If you reach this point, and feel like you can no longer continue, at least you reached the point you were willing to get to. While you might not have achieved total success, by recognizing your Quit Ability Point, you have reached your own personal measure of success. I have always found it easier to set the quit ability point at the beginning of a task as it is always a lot higher than if you did it later on. For example, if you decide before you go to the gym what you are going to do and how long you will do it before you go, you will have more chance of doing it than if you just go there without a plan.

This reminds me of when I was buying my Aston Martin a few years ago. I did my research, I had the price I was prepared to pay and if they didn't give it to me at that price, then I was walking away...... I got it.

Once you know how far you are prepared to go, it makes the journey and the challenges easier.

Planning Ahead: Know Where You Want to Go

Life can be a very exciting adventure. However, our lives can change dramatically and expectantly. Sometimes, we might lose a job or a loved one. Other people have very positive changes which come expectantly. As an example, meeting your future wife or husband, winning the lottery, or being on TV. Because life throws us curveballs from time to time, it is important to plan for change and embrace it and evolve.

Planning for change is a bit of an oxymoron. You can never predict change, especially when it is unexpected. However, there are a few tactics we can embrace when dramatic changes do take place. Firstly, when an unexpected change occurs in your life, you need to re-examine your current list of goals. You need to have an honest discussion with yourself in terms of your ability to see the goal to its end. With this said, you also need to examine whether your goals must change dramatically because of the dramatic, unexpected change. When unplanned changed occurs, make sure to take the time to reflect on how this change will affect and influence your current course. Failure to do so can lead to larger hurdles and setbacks: remember what Einstein said, "in the middle of every difficulty lies opportunity." Make sure you look for the opportunities.

Sometimes, you can plan for change in a very accurate way. For instance, if you open a business, you need to look at the worst possible outcome and prepare for it. What's your Plan B? While you do not want to think of failure when you first open a business, you need to plan for the worst case scenario. When people start a business, they often say, "I will not fail", so they will not plan for failure or things not going according to plan. While it is important to have 100% confidence when you open a business, it is also important that you look at all of the pros and cons, get professional advice, understand the risks and competition. For example, just because you are a great chef, doesn't mean you can run a profitable restaurant. Be diligent and be honest with yourself.

In many ways, planning for change involves KNOWING how to deal with change. In the Why Factor, we deal with change all the time. For this reason, we are interested in managing our expectations of change. **By learning how to manage change, we learn how to move through life in a positive and dynamic way.** A simple way is to ask why the change, understand it and come up with a new plan of action.

No matter where you are in the Why Factor Academy, as a "Why Not Me?" person, you need to always be planning ahead. You need to plan your goals ahead of time, understand how to reach your goals, as well as the cost of achieving those goals. In many ways, you need to learn to fully organise your life. **Life is like one big chess game**, you always need to be a few steps ahead and have a counter attack plan or defence.

LIFE IS LIKE A CHESS GAME. I NEED
TO BE 3/4 STEPS AHEAD OF MY LIFE PLAN

To correctly plan ahead, you should always
make sure to write lists. It is easy to forget a
list in your mind, but it is hard to throw away
your thoughts when they are on paper, so

it is a good idea to make lists whenever relevant. For instance, you might make a list to cover the tasks for the day. Go to the grocery store, have the car fixed, and pick up the laundry, to name a few daily tasks. What you really need is a list of things that need to be done today that will move you toward your goal. Beyond this daily list, try and make a weekly list. Again, the things that will move you toward your goal. You might want to make lists in terms of three months, six months, one year, etc. We will cover this in detail later. Here, you can clearly state your goals, as well as list the costs in terms of money and time. As you achieve a goal within any given time frame, being able to mark the item off your list of goals is a great feeling. So make lists whenever possible.

Self-Reflection

Within the Why Factor, it is important to always self-reflect. In other words, you need to constantly be honest with yourself. For instance, it is important to reflect on your day to day life, but you need to also reflect on the larger picture. I like going for a walk in the countryside to reflect. As you move through life, you need to reflect on the important points of pivot. Meaning, you need to reflect from points A to B, B to C, and A to Z.

Always find quiet time to reflect, we live in such a busy and noisy world today that sometimes we can't think.

Always ask yourself these power questions. **"Is what I'm doing working?" "Is my business working?" "Is my relationship working?"** and be honest with yourself.

"IS WHAT IM DOING WORKING?"

Self reflection is not a linear process. Instead, you need to self-reflect on a daily basis. Beyond reflecting on your day, you need to reflect on your weekly actions. Beyond the weekly reflection, it is important to consider how you have improved over the course of a year. Recognise these improvements and compliment yourself on moving forward. Next, consider the five year reflection period, the ten year reflection period, and so on. Within the Why Factor, self reflection, and honesty within your self-reflection process, is a critical tool for long term success.

What Lifestyle Do You Want To Live

Before you decide your goals, a great way to reflect upon your current thoughts, in fact your long term dreams, is to ask yourself the type of lifestyle you want to live. For instance, if you want to spend your summers on the Riviera, you need to choose a career path which will allow you to afford the Riviera lifestyle. If you want to drive a BMW, Jaguar or Mercedes etc., you need to determine which jobs or careers will pay you the type of money you need to drive the car you want.

The biggest challenge is making the decision to live a better lifestyle. Having clarity on where you want to go, what you want to do. Beyond this, you need to put the **plan together and work the plan**.

The job you do is equal to the money you make. This limits the lifestyle we can live. If you want to make £100,000 a year, you need to understand what you need to do to make this money. Will opening a cleaning business make you £100,000? Or do you need to employ a number of people to meet your goal of making £100,000? You need an understanding of the lifestyle you want and how to get there. Schools do not teach this.

Many people would rather spend their days biking around town, and that is certainly a worthy and noble lifestyle. Remember, money is not the key to success in the Why Factor Academy. Instead, happiness is the best measure of success. For this reason, your goals in life might revolve around a passion which will not allow you to summer in the Hamptons. For this reason, you need to understand the lifestyle you want to live before you begin to act on your goals.

As you can tell, there are many requirements of the "Why, Why Not Me?" type of mentality. All of the characteristics of a "Why, Why Not Me?" person are positive, and they are also the types of people who are willing to work hard for their success. Remember, the "Why, Why Not Me?" type of person does not fit into a single form of success. Instead, the "Why, Why Not Me?" person is a complex person who has a few very similar traits. They work hard, understand failure, and act quickly, and so on. "Why, Why Not Me?" people say enough is enough and stand up and fight for their life and success. As we move through the remainder of the book, you will learn more important qualities of the "Why, Why Not Me?" type of person.

THE WANDERERS

When we speak about the inactive "Why, Why Not Me?" type of person, we are often very close to the descriptor of a wanderer. Wanderers have the ability to achieve greatness, but instead of achieving their goals, they wander around the world, never acting on their talents or abilities. For this reason, it is a good idea to spend a bit of time discussing how a wanderer is different than a "Why, Why Not Me?" person. The difference between a Wanderer and the "Why Not Me?" person is the Why Factor, they don't ask the "Why?" questions. When I speak to people who have been successful at times, they tend to explain how close they were to becoming successful, only to watch the success drift away. They reach a cliff and plunge over the side of the cliff. This happens to a lot of people. And some people give up on their aspirations, sort of telling themselves to walk away, no point going through that again. Again this reminds us of the story with the elephant and the Banyan tree.

Who Are the Wanderers?

One of the most talented and yet the most unfortunate group of people in the world are the people who never ask themselves the question "Why?" They never question where they are in their lives. Instead, they simply tend to wander through life with a certain degree of ignorant bliss. Some wanderers are happy and there is nothing wrong drifting through life from childhood till the day they find themselves being placed in the grave. Other Wanderers are not happy but just go with the flow. It is easier to wander with the group than charter a different course, that's why it can be difficult to break out.

Other times, a wanderer reaches a point in life where they ask themselves the question "Why, Why Me?" It's still not a great place to be in life, but at least it's a step up from the wanderer stage.

Do YOU NEED MORE?

Sometimes, a wanderer finally reaches the point of being tired of drifting from job-to-job or day-to-day. Other times, a wanderer is forced to change because of some tragedy, death in the family, work redundancy, and so on. From these unfortunate events, they ask themselves the question "Why, Why Me?" In time, they might begin to ask themselves the question, "Why, Why Not Me?" With this said, they might not act on their desire to change. Then, one day, they might finally take the corrective actions to start changing their miseries. In a sense, they become a member of the Why Factor Academy. Remember, this is a path I experienced, starting as a teenager, and ending with the person you see today.

A wanderer does not have the drive to act on their path to success or are afraid of running away from the group and being different, which is one of the greatest differences between the wanderers and the "Why, Why Not Me?" people. Make sure to constantly act on the things you are passionate about. Beyond acting on your passions, you need to always remember to never give up. If you give up, you become a wanderer. If you have all the qualities of a "Why, Why Not Me?" person, but lack the motivation to learn or change, you are not a "Why, Why Not Me?" person, you are a wanderer.

Wanderers generally do not have any goals, aspirations or direction. They do not want to succeed or add to the quality of their lives. Instead, they are quite happy with what they are given freely. They are not willing to work for their success. You see, society, education and the Government create this group because you can't have everyone wanting to succeed can you? The Why Factor Academy is not criticising this group but giving you the tools to break free and get what you truly deserve, if you want it. That's a key, do you really want it?

The Wanderers tend to be people who have given up the chase and accepted where they are. A good test is to tell other fellow wanderers that you are thinking of going back to university, starting a new career or starting your own business and listen to their answers... they will spend most of the time telling you to stay where you are, it won't work, it can't be done etc. That's why to break free you will have to change some of your friends and associates otherwise they will pull you down.

In my earlier days, I was repeatedly told "Why bother? Just accept where you are... stop trying to be something you're not... you think you are better than us... why don't you first get a regular job?"

As I said earlier, I was a wanderer too until I realised and this is important. **I was brought up to believe that people were better than me as opposed to "Why they were better or different to me."** Once you understand this concept, your self-esteem will grow stronger every day.

CHAPTER 7

THE MASK - THE PROBLEM

O ur belief system is how we see ourselves. What do we mean by our belief system? The beliefs that you have today, true or false. For example, beliefs about food, society, education, parenting, your abilities, looks, relationships and ambitions, to mention a few, are a sum total of you and the way you act or respond to life. Our belief system can act as a screen or mask in which we look at the world. These masks influence the decisions that we make or don't make. For example, some of the negative masks include, *"I hate my job, I don't love my partner, I am unlucky, I am not good enough,"* etc.

Your belief system is your control tower. **Once you believe something to be true or false, but you really believe it with passion and your conscious mind accepts it, your subconscious mind will obey and deliver.** For example, if you believe you are clumsy, then your subconscious will work to make sure you are clumsy and stay that way.

"YOUR BELIEF SYSTEM IS YOUR CONTROL TOWER"

It is so important to understand the mask you have acquired. The good, the bad and the ugly masks (beliefs). Keep the good, change the bad and get rid of the ugly masks (beliefs). This is a lifelong, never ending project on yourself because as you get rid of your masks, you sometimes acquire new ones; which is why you need to constantly keep on reviewing yourself.

As you enter the Why Factor Academy, you need to recognise that people wear masks. We all wear masks. Sometimes we need to wear masks to protect ourselves. Whether we are on the metro, the bus, in stores or at work, people are always wearing masks. In many ways, people wear masks to hide their own problems. People wear masks to make themselves seem more positive or successful than they really are. No matter if the mask is positive or negative; masks can be a tricky area of the Why Factor to navigate. What I mean by that is, if you have a self-limiting belief, we will have to deal with it before we can go past and grow.

You see life through your belief system. Whatever your belief (mask) about yourself, if you believe it to be true then it will be true for you. Consider plastic surgery, for example. There are many people today getting plastic surgery because they don't like what they see in the mirror. They believe that they need it, etc., and even when they ask their friends and are told they are beautiful, still their belief system says they are not right and they need it.

WE SEE OUR LIFE THROUGH OUR BELIEF SYSTEM (MASK)

You don't know where we get this negative belief from. We tend to get some of our negative beliefs as kids, and they grow and manifest in time. **The challenge we have is our mask controls our lives unconsciously.** For example, you have a belief that you are no good at maths, and when asked a maths question, you say that you are not good at numbers. It's not that you are bad with numbers, but you have told yourself so many times that you are not good at numbers that you now believe it. What you need to do is start questioning the belief and say, "Why? Why I am not good at numbers, what is causing this?" It's the Elephant excuse again...

In the Why Factor Academy, it is important to remember that everyone wears a mask. Every one of us has baggage that we carry around and we need to get rid of the baggage to grow. I am still getting rid of some excess baggage, but again it's being aware and dealing with it. In other words, everyone puts on a front which hides our true feelings and emotions. As an example, acting confidently when you are not. Or, acting happy when you are not. It's a facade we all wear, and simply put, we all wear masks, the good masks are okay but the negative, bad and ugly ones hold us back. Think about it, nobody really knows what you are thinking. One of the biggest masks (beliefs) we wear that hold us back is, "I'm not good enough". I struggled with that one for many years.

Only those who are close to us can see through the masks we wear. Mothers are great, they can see right through you. In fact, they only need to hear your voice on the phone and they know something is wrong. Surely, it is easier to see when your family members are angry when compared to a stranger on the streets. At the office, it can be easy to look beyond someone's work mask, but difficult to penetrate the masks of their personal lives.

Beyond understanding how other people wear masks, we need to spend time understanding the masks that we wear. Once we understand the masks that we wear, we can begin to change the negative ones for a more positive belief, which will then increase our success. This is now self-development, making a better, wholesome you. This then allows you to deal with challenges differently, which in turn changes your beliefs, which will then change your future in the right direction.

The masks that we wear are like a TV screen we look through. Anything that happens to us in our lives has to go through this mask: it has to go through our belief system. Our mask beliefs control how we see life and when we react to events in our life. Something happens, your belief system analyses it, and if it agrees it lets it in, and if it doesn't agree then it will reject it. For example, "I can't do it." Once your belief tells you that you can't do something, and then you approach the task in hand, you automatically say, "I can't do it." It is our belief systems which decide how we wear our masks as well as the types of masks we wear, positive or negative.

A lot of times when we are young, we are told that we are not good enough. It is drilled into our heads until we believe it. We not only begin to believe we are not good enough, we accept that we are not good enough. Even if someone pays us a compliment, but our belief system says I am not good enough (even if our inner thoughts were to says, "yes if only they knew this about me!!") our brains will never get the positive message. So, keeping positive beliefs is a battle that we need to constantly fight. We need to remove the negative connotations from our surroundings and our minds. But this process is not a one-time saying. We need to constantly tell ourselves that we are good enough, that we can succeed, and that we are worth the effort to succeed. In other **words it's important that you believe in yourself...Why Not?**

Understanding How We Function

It is important to remember that **your belief system can imprison you or empower you.** If you are constantly surrounded by negative people, your belief system is sure to imprison you. If you are surrounded by positive people, you are much more likely to feel empowered. For this reason, it is important to understand the difference between being positively empowered and negatively imprisoned.

I CAN DO ANYTHING ATTITUDE.

In terms of positive empowerment, some people are very lucky to be surrounded by this sort of environment from birth. Most people, however, are exposed to negative comments and criticism from a young age. In either case, you need to constantly remind yourself to think positively, as well as remind yourself to be surrounded by positive people. In many ways, the closer someone is to you, the more positive they should be.

Your immediate family and the people you associate with should be quite positive, while the people on the fringe of your life are allowed to be less positive (since they spend very little time in your life). In order to keep a positive home, it is important to remain positive yourself. In other words, you need to remember that you are a member of a positive group, not the centre of positive energy. With this said, you should never need to wear the mask of denial when it comes to being positively empowered. Meaning, make sure to be honest when it comes to your positive mentality. Don't just blindly believe that you are positive; ask yourself constantly if you are truly positive, or just acting positive for the sake of others. Remember, masks are hard to judge. **The more real you become; the happier you are as a person.** It is also important that no one is perfect, so we are not looking for 100% to believe in ourselves, just for you to start believing in yourself now!

Once you have established a truly positive relationship with yourself and your surroundings, you can begin to feel empowered. Sometimes, being empowered involves taking on a more challenging goal in your life. Perhaps it's going back to school, running a marathon, changing careers, finally opening a business, and so on. As we discussed, you need to approach empowerment from a realistic perspective.

For this reason, you need to avoid negative triggers. You need to make sure you remove any negative triggers from your lives, before they overtake your ability to succeed, or your desire to succeed. The people you associate with or believe in can be responsible for up to 80% of your success.

Some of the masks (beliefs) we wear, we wear as a protection for our innermost feelings.

The Masks People Wear

1. The Obnoxious Mask

The people who wear the mask of being obnoxious hide behind a mask of intense insecurity. They tend to think that their opinions are more important than anyone else's' in the room, and treat people accordingly.

2. The Dunce Mask (I'm not good enough)

People who wear the dunce mask are the people who act stupid or never question why they feel that way. Society and education have created this but because they don't know why, they use this as an excuse, as to why people should not expect them to excel. Unfortunately, people who have bought into this mask don't seek better jobs and careers.

3. The Holier than Thou Mask (We are better than you)

These people who wear the holier than thou mask are sometimes hiding the fact that they often have the most moral problems to hide. It is sad to see this as it goes against the true value of religion. For this reason, it's important to stay away from these people as much as you can. Some politicians often wear this mask.

4. The Drama Queen / King (I'm important and need attention)

We have all met people like this. Always needing to be the centre of attention. In fact, many professional people, for example, male and female actors, and office managers, bosses, etc., are drama kings and queens. The next time you meet one, ask yourself why they are like that. It's amazing - you will begin to see a different side to them, and also what they are hiding.

5. The Pessimist Mask

Some people are always negative. The Pessimist Mask people are constantly cynical. They are the sort of people who will, when it's a nice day and you greet them with "it's a nice day", will reply, "Is it?" The Why Me people tend to wear the pessimist mask the most. They say the only good thing about a pessimist is that if we borrow money from them and don't pay them back, it doesn't matter as they were not expecting you to pay them back anyway!!!

6. The Passive-Aggressive Mask

Passive Aggressive people pass their rage and anger through subtle messages for example, emails and recommendations. They take it out on their family and not the people who angered them. They like to point out all of their pet peeves, and seek to change the world to suit their own, insecure ideals. Think of the people who leave notes around the office refrigerator, or makes sly innuendos or remarks, as a great example of a passive aggressive person.

7. The Mask of Comedy (Don't take life too seriously)

Many people like to portray an outlook on life by making a comedy of every conversation and circumstance. To make themselves feel better, and to hide from their own insecurities, they try to make a comedy out of every experience, person or situation. They laugh it off and laugh life off, never learning and growing. How many comedians have you heard of that have been depressed? Making other people laugh and being happy in ones' self are two different things. I know because I always used to wear this mask.

8. The Guru Mask

People who appear to be "know-it-alls" for the most part just have a belief system that they are better than everyone else and know it all. They just happen to know a lot of trivia about many unrelated facts – but rarely any information that is of any useful value. They want to be respected, but need to understand that respect is something you earn.

9. The Intellectual Mask (I am intelligent)

Intellect can be a great quality, but being too intellectual around others can be a sign of a lack of intellect. An intellectual will often draw on their genuine expertise in a certain area during conversations to impress people. They use quoting statements and event examples to back up their points, in order to make sure that others feel inferior. They tend to be very anal, and fearful of failure.

10. The Politically Correct

The Politically Correct people say the things that they think you want to hear and try to avoid creating confrontations. They make decisions based on the situation. People who wear the mask of political correctness are too aware of the world's faults and play for the popular vote, but are severely unaware of their own thoughts. They live in the politically right or wrong world with a lot of grey areas.

11. The Cash / No Cash Mask

Don't let the fancy suit, car and house fool you. While they talk the talk, when it comes to finance, the banks do all the talking for them. Meaning, they are cash poor and appearance wealthy. They might make a great salary, but most of this money goes towards the rent and credit card finance charges. I recently heard an expression when I was in Dallas, Texas; they called them "big hat, no cattle." I use the term, "cash with no cash people". You see them in public places showing off, trying to impress people who do not care. Crazy! For this reason, you need to question whether someone is genuinely successful or wearing an impressive mask of success. Don't get me wrong we need to dress to impress, but you don't need to go into major debt to do this.

12. The Mask of Friendship

Many times, the people who you think are friends are clearly not friends at all. We have all had someone who we thought was a friend and they let us down. They are only interested in spending time around you because they feel there is a financial or other benefit to them. Other times, they are around you in order to share your life story through gossip with other friends. For this reason, you really need to make sure the people closest to you are truly your friends. Real friends are the ones who, when you say you want to do something like changing career, for example, will encourage and support you. They care for you when you are down and motivate you.

There are so many masks that after a while it is fun detecting new ones. The key is always to ask yourself why they - or you - are wearing that mask and what is going on in their lives - or your life.

Why We Wear Masks

Some of the masks we create are a camouflage, a sum of the problems we have created in our lives, either positive or negative. For example, *"I didn't get a good education that's why I can't move forward. I am a good cook but really I can only cook one dish, , I am confident because I don't want to show how vulnerable I am, I am happy but really I am not happy, etc."*

We wear masks because we have no choice but to wear masks; society and education teaches us to. Also, we wear some masks to protect our feelings, it is important to not share all of our problems with the outside world, since we need to take responsibility for our own mistakes. We need to make sure we do not bring down others with our misery, in the same way we cannot allow others to bring us into their misery. For this reason, wearing masks can be a positive thing too.

Sometimes, when our personal lives are going through a bit of a rut, we need to wear a mask at work to avoid anyone finding out. My mother always used to say that **you should never do your dirty washing in public.** A good example is when you see a couple split or get divorced and people say, "I thought you were getting on really well?" They were wearing a mask, pretending all was well, when it was not. We also need to make sure our personal lives do not inhibit our ability to succeed in business. We wear masks because our biology requires us to wear masks. For this reason, it is difficult to not wear a mask at some point in the day or at least to be in control consciously when you are wearing or not wearing a mask. A challenge is removing the mask, being genuine and sincere with yourself, your partner and especially to people who are close to you. This will help you become a better you, you need to learn to like and accept you. **The more you learn to like yourself and believe in yourself, the fewer masks you wear.** Brian Tracy teaches us to use the affirmation: I like myself, I like myself. When you say 'I like myself', how do you feel? Your feelings will tell you what mask you are wearing.

If we are frustrated at home, surely, it is important to be honest with your partner and find solutions to your problems. But what we do is wear a mask or two as we solve the problem. So, when dealing with home issues, you might wear a mask from time-to-time which is somewhat negative. If you have children, they are watching and learning from you how to put your mask beliefs on.

It is important to remember that your belief system, if negative, can imprison and hold you back; and if positive, can empower you. If you are constantly surrounded by negative people, your belief system is sure to imprison you. If you are surrounded by positive people, you are much more likely to feel empowered. For this reason, it is important to understand to strive at all times to be positively empowered by having positive thoughts and positive beliefs of the outcome.

Living in Denial

Denial, as they say, is not just a river anymore. People live in denial. They tell themselves they are better than they really are, they live above their means. They buy into a story which is false. Sometimes, you need to look in the mirror and admit that you messed up in an honest and positive way.

Even I wear the mask of denial sometimes. As an example, one business I started involved a large building I built. There were two buildings 7,500 square feet on a one acre lot. The building had all the bells and whistles, security, etc. It was purpose built; my business was flying at the time. Then there were some outside factors that changed and the company started to recede to the point that there were just two people in 3,500sq foot of office, me and my general manager. I was in denial believing I was going to build it back.

One day, among the more miserable days of this business, I was staring out of the window looking at my Jaguar XKR Super Charger and I said to myself, "Ayo, you have to be honest with yourself, stop kidding yourself, you do not have the business that you used to have, and the business has changed."

You have to take a step back, and look at yourself, regroup and attack. You can't go forward until you are real with yourself. I was living in a state of denial. However, I was lucky to realise my state of denial, and was able to move on and rebuild a profitable business. Such is life. Once you catch yourself in denial you need to take action immediately. Denial camouflages the problem so you can't find a solution and act on it.

Removing Negative and Ego Centred Masks

Get rid of any negative, self-limiting masks: I can't do it, I'm not smart enough, etc. Get rid of an egoistic mask (chip on the shoulder) and replace it with positive self-belief and with humbleness. The negative mask will force you to move from the active, Why, Why Not Me mentality to the inactive, Why, Why

Not Me mentality. If you continue to remain negative, you might finally find yourself as a Wanderer, lost in your job, giving up on your ambitions to succeed.

Besides the negative mask, the ego-driven mask can do an equal amount of damage. People who wear the ego mask are not very honest with themselves, so they tend to remain stuck in the Why, Why Me mentality, or they live in a false sense of the Why, Why Not Me mentality. Remember, you need to be honest with yourself, which requires a large dose of humility. If you wear an ego-centric mask, you cannot have an honest conversation with yourself, your progress or surroundings. For this reason, make sure to remove the ego mask if you would like to find success in the Why Factor Academy. There is a certain amount of ego you need, but too much is not good. Too big an ego will keep you in denial. **Your ego will make you and your ego will break you.**

CHAPTER 8

THE INNER YOU VERSUS THE OUTER YOU

Within the Why Factor, there are two distinct branches. The first branch is the Inner You, while the second branch is the Outer You. When they merge, you get the stem, the harmony.

You get the balance of what is going on in the brain and how the world perceives you. You need to re-evaluate why you are the person you are. Why do I think the way I think? What are the negative remarks which come from my mind? You are re-programming your brain to say these things.

Where did you get the impression that you were not good at music? It's a psychological scar we carry for no reason.

So I needed to find a profession with stability and I needed to find a profession which would train me. Plumbing and carpentry were not my type of work. So I got into sales, but I never thought of myself as a sales person. Now, I am a successful and happy person. But if I had never asked myself why, I would not be in this position. **I used to think all the problems and challenges were out there, but then I realised that they are all in my brain**. So I started re-programming my brain until a new set of positive belief systems, like, "Nobody is better than you, just ahead of you." If you are prepared to listen, learn and apply your new positive belief system, you too can achieve it: "Why? Why Not Me?"

ALL MY CHALLENGES ARE NOT OUT THERE, THEY ARE IN MY BRAIN.

An immature mind said to me once, "Ayo you are brain washing me... I said yes I am. I realised many years ago that **you can be brain washed to succeed or brainwashed to fail.** Either way you are being brainwashed so choose wisely.

Why the Problem

Inner You versus Outer You. Most people think the problem is outside, but the problem is internal. We are used to blaming our families, boss, partners, yourself, you name it. Instead, we need to think, analyse and process information. There is two of you,

you and how your brain thinks. Part of your brain is always agreeing with something or someone, while another part of the brain is disagreeing. So you need to remember, the inner you controls the outer you, so you need to take control of your thoughts. **Control your thoughts, control your world.** Earl Nightingale said, "You are what you think about all day..." You are today a sum total of your thoughts. Your thoughts today are a preview of your future. **Change your thinking, change your future...**

Your thoughts become your words, your words become your actions, your actions become your habits, and your habits become your character and your character controls your destiny. And it all starts with a thought.

Work On the Inner You

This is where you really win the lottery. This is the key to your success and happiness.

Work on the inner you and how to continuously improve. Discover how to recognize when and how to improve. We have been brought up in society to focus on the outer you but the key to success is gaining control of the inner you.

The inner you is referring to your thoughts, your thinking and how you process the information you receive, positive or negative. It is the real you. The way you work on the inner you is to talk to yourself using positive, personal and present tense affirmations like, "I can do it", "I am responsible for my success. I live in a nice house, everything I touch is a success, etc." Every time you have a negative thought, replace it with a positive affirmation.

Recognize the Outer You

How to be honest with yourself. When to reflect on your present, past and future. The outer you is all the baggage you have collected; the good, the bad and the ugly. It needs sorting in order to get rid of the bad and ugly bits. Again, the way you do that is to constantly challenge your thoughts and ask "Why?" "Why am I thinking that way?" "Where did that belief come from, is it a genuine belief or a false one created by myself?" This changes the negative, pessimist thoughts to positive, optimistic thoughts.

The Inner/Outer Balance

The more you align the inner you with the outer you, the more fulfilled you become as a human being. Achieving harmony and balance between the inner you and outer you is one of the main keys to happiness and success. Enjoy your new journey of discovering the real you.

Taking Care of Your Thoughts and Words

Now you understand that your outer you is a reflection of your thoughts and thinking, it is important that, when going forward, you question those thoughts by asking the "Why?" question. "Why am I thinking these thoughts?" Drill them down to find out where they have come from and replace the negative beliefs with positive ones. For example, "I'm not good enough" should be replaced with "I can do anything I put my mind to." "I'm not good at remembering names" replaced with "I'm good at remembering names. **Take control of your thoughts and take control of your life.**" Exciting isn't it?

CHAPTER 9

THE OPTIMISTS VERSUS THE PESSIMISTS

In life, you will find that there are two types of people. One group is comprised of optimists, while the other group is full of pessimists. Beyond these two groups of people, I find there are three colours of people in the world. Green, Amber and Red. In this chapter, we will discuss how these colours relate to people, and how people move from red to amber or from amber to green.

Some people just see the difficulty in every situation; they are ingrained with their

163

ideals. Nothing is for the better, you hear them say, "be careful, are you sure?" These tend to be the negative, red people who are the pessimists. Then the green people are the optimists who are more likely to say, "I can do this, it's achievable," etc. The optimists are focused and keep moving forward towards their goals. Then you have the amber people, the people who are between these two extremes. Sometimes, they will be positive, sometimes, they will be negative. They are only as good as the people and circumstances they are around at the time. You need to decide which one of these three people you are. Beyond this simple statement, you need to recognize which colour of person you are, and when you need to change.

Traffic Lights

Our brain functions like traffic lights; red, amber and green. At times, we find ourselves stopped at an intersection, not able to cross the road or change paths. Some people never leave the intersection, but are constantly trapped at the lights. Other people tend to find themselves in the amber. On a traffic light, the amber means caution, slow down or get ready to go. Many people who live in the amber for too long tend to get into accidents in their lives, "do I go or do I stay?" They are indecisive and don't reflect or observe their world, so they are prone to danger. When the light goes to amber, they panic and think "should I go or should I stay?" they are indecisive.

Finally, the green light people are those who don't slow down and are free to cross the intersection smoothly. However, this type of person does not reach green lights by accident. Instead, they make the correct decisions in order to find the green lights. Their timing is always great, because they study their personal traffic patterns. They are cautious when they need to be cautious, and take calculated risks when they need to take risks.

When something happens, the red people say "Stop! Don't do anything" as they think the worst of situations. Green people are focused and keep moving forward toward their goals. Green people, even on a red light, are looking for ways to cross the intersection and, as soon as the lights change, they are ready for action. However, the amber people are indecisive and follow the red people; unless they are in the car with the green people and they have no choice than to go along with their decisions.

Three Colours of People

When considering the colours of people, the red people are hard to change, but we need to change them to amber first, before we can turn them to green and keep them on green. For those that are amber, we need to teach them to turn to the green. And once we realise this transition, we can make positive changes to how we are and our surroundings. This will help you with dealing with people and how you can influence and help them.

The three colours of people are very similar to a traffic light and life in general. When you are in the red, you are stopped at the light, letting life pass you by. When you are stuck in the amber, you have the ability to move forward, but you do so with caution. When you are in the green, you are free to go anywhere and to have what you want in life. It's smooth sailing. For this reason, it is helpful to think of a traffic light when it comes to deciding which colour person you are at the moment. Red, Amber or Green.

When I am talking to someone on a one-to-one basis, I take in the entire experience and I use it. The reason why I use this experience is simple. The easiest way to communicate with people is to paint pictures, and taking in the experience of communicating with different types of people allows you to paint a lot of types of paintings. **The brain does not think in terms of words, it thinks in terms of pictures.** So, most people get hung up on words. Instead, you need to remember the picture. **A picture is worth a thousand words.**

Think of an Elephant. When you think of an elephant, you do not think of the letters on the page: E.L.E.P.H.A.N.T, you think of the image of an elephant. So, in communication, use words to present clear pictures of what you are trying to say.

The Red People: The Pessimists

I have always said if you are going to borrow money, borrow it from a pessimist because they never think they will get it back. They are too negative. They never have the expectation of doing well, of things working according to schedule, and so on. People who are pessimistic tend to move through life stuck at the stop sign. For this reason, we need to make sure we do not spend our lives surrounded by those in the red.

This reminds me of a story that I heard; about a priest on his way home who sees a guy on the side of a bridge. The man wants to jump, but the priest eventually convinces the man to come down from the bridge and to go and get a cup of coffee. The man and the priest talk for another two hours. After two hours they both go back to the bridge and both jump off... This is a great way of looking at how a pessimist can negatively affect us. I don't care how positive you think you are, if you spend too much time around pessimists, you will fail. Their brain is on red, nothing is possible in their world.

The Amber People: Living between the Positive and Negative

There are a group of people who are neither green nor red. Instead, this group of people live between the two colours. They live between the positive and negative. They make progress on certain days, and step backwards on others. In many ways, the Amber people are the wanderers of the world.

Amber people can be complex. In fact, we all tend to spend most of our time in the amber part of the spectrum. We are constantly striving to live in the green, and doing our best to avoid the red. However, we never go directly from green to red or red to green. Instead, we tend to spend a lot of time in the amber.

Some people are constantly stuck in the amber. These people tend to have many highs and lows. Not just in life, but highs and low through the course of a single day. During the morning, they can be filled with the colour red, and as night approaches, they might turn greener. For those stuck in the amber often, a lot of discipline is needed to make sure they move and stick to the green.

When you find yourself in the amber part of the spectrum, you need to determine why you are stuck in a cycle of up and down. Remember, you need to have an honest conversation with yourself, "Why? Why Not Me?" in order to move out of the amber and into the green. If you do not have an honest conversation with yourself, you will find yourself slipping from the amber to the red. For this reason, being honest with yourself and reflecting on your current state is exceptionally important.

The Green People: The Optimists

The green people of the world are the optimists. Optimists have a mental attitude and world view which is constantly positive. They never view the glass as being half empty; they only see the glass as being half full. In the Why Factor Academy, you need to remain a green person, but you also have to know when to recognize you are not being a green person. In many ways, no one remains a green person forever. Sometimes the lights are on red, but if you know you are a green person, the light will change back to green very soon. We need to learn how to change the traffic light as we move through life.

Being green has nothing to do with how you live or how much money you have. I have seen people who are poor and happy. I have seen rich people who are not happy. **Money does not buy you happiness.** So at first, you need to be a happy person. **To be a happy person, you need to be an optimist and like yourself.** Remember, green means go and it means you are growing. I like the American expression "I'm good to go." Wow! What a powerful statement, full of positive energy.

Green people are the happy people, the feel-good people, and the people you want to be around. These are the people who see challenges as stepping stones to success and understand that it is part of the journey that will make them stronger and more successful.

Changing the Colour from Red to Amber or Amber to Green

Remember, while it might seem like you are stuck in a certain colour, this is never the case; it's your thinking that is stuck. You can always move from the red to the amber and the amber to the green. With this said, the slope can be negative as well. You can move from the green, down to the amber, and fall to the red. For this reason, you need to constantly ask yourself in which direction you are moving, and whether or not the direction you are moving in is towards the green. Once you are in the green, you need to stay in this area for as long as possible. Remember, green means go, so the more time we spend in the green, the more successful we will be at the end of our lives. To stay in the green, you need to ask yourself what is working for you and why it's working, then capture the answer and keep on repeating the answer and that will keep you green. If you spend too much time in the red, you will one day reflect on your life and find you are full of regret, never making the moves to succeed when the opportunity presented itself. If you live in the amber, you might look back at life as various shades of grey, but you will still be looking towards the aspects of your life which did not go well. In other words, you will always reflect on the life in terms of what you did not achieve or did not do. I remember someone saying to me once that the only things you regret in life are the things you never did.

Maintaining the Green

When it comes to the colour of your personality, your ultimate goal is to live a life maintaining the green. Whilst you are sure to reach an amber or red light from time to time, your goal should be to maintain as many green lights as possible. By following the Why Factor, you are well on your way to maintaining green lights.

Another main key to staying green is to mix with as many Green people as possible and make sure the people you are associated with are green people.

In order to maintain green lights, you need to recognize when you are moving towards the amber. Ask yourself "Why?" and what is causing it and then change. This conversation will see you head back to green. You also need to make sure you never put yourself in a difficult situation which might force you into the red side of the spectrum. What I am giving you is a simple analogy so you can catch yourself and keep you moving forward with your goals. This will also to help you to identify the people to avoid or navigate around.

RED

AMBER

GREEN

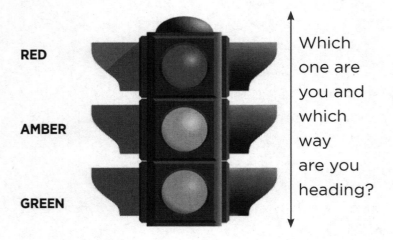

Which one are you and which way are you heading?

Are you good to go?

THE PLEASURE PAIN PRINCIPLE

The pleasure-pain principle was discovered by Sigmund Freud in the 1920s. The pleasure-pain principle **is the instinctual seeking of pleasure and avoidance of pain in order to satisfy biological and psychological needs.** In other words, we have been pre-programmed with an inbuilt instinct to seek pleasure and avoid pain. We move from what is painful to what is pleasurable. Wow, did you get it? Please read again, this is so powerful....

As humans, we move from pain to pleasure and pleasure to pain. Our lives operate between these two emotions. **Our experiences of pain and pleasure act as**

references for our belief system to reflect on. If we are working in a job that is not taking us anywhere, the point of change comes when it becomes more painful to continue doing the job than to find a new job. At this point we start looking for a new job, in other words we move from pain to pleasure. Another example is if you have toothache but don't go to the dentist until the toothache is more painful than the fear of being in the dentist chair. Another example: if you are overweight, the pain of losing weight is harder than the pleasure of eating cakes and sweets. So we carry on eating the cakes and sweets.

The key point to understanding this is that the **pleasure-pain principle discovered by Freud has already been biologically programmed into us and behaves as a natural instinct to which we subconsciously perform.** Wow! When I first got this, I began to understand why in certain areas I wasn't improving because where I was at, was pleasure and where I wanted to go looked like pain. It's amazing. Sometimes we are stuck in a rut but the pain of changing to get out of the rut is more than the pain of staying in the rut; so we don't change. Does that make sense? It's just like going from a warm room to outside on a cold, breezy wintery day. You only do it because you have to... right? Well so it is with us, we only change when we have to. Once you get this concept, you will understand what successful people do is that they **override the pain by turning the pain of change, the action needed, etc., into pleasure and then once your conscious buys into it, your subconscious goes to work to achieve it.** Do you get it?

People then admire you for your success, instead of understanding why and how you did it.

Successful people understand pain. They understand that's where the success is, it's breaking the pain barrier. They tend to leave their comfort zone and take calculated risks. They learn from these risks. If you are not prepared to do this, endure the pain of moving from being unsuccessful to successful, then you will never achieve your goals.

Understanding what motivates you is the key to the pleasure-pain principle. Everything you do is motivated by two fundamental desires; one is to gain pleasure and the other is to avoid pain. This has also been described as the motivation of comfort vs. discomfort, or love vs. fear. Think about any decision you have made in your life. You ultimately made the decision to do anything based on **your desire to either obtain some form of pleasure or avoid some form of pain.**

Think of the extent we go to for love, which is ultimate pleasure and think of the extent we go to, to avoid the things we fear?

As you go about your day, you are making decisions, either consciously or unconsciously. And as you make each decision about what to do and what not to do, you are asking and answering the pleasure vs. pain question. It does not matter if you are making a decision as simple as what to have for lunch or as life-altering as proposing marriage, your decisions are based on your assessment of what will help you to gain pleasure and what will help you to avoid pain.

The scary part is all this is going on unconsciously. Well no more! This is your wakeup call from the Why Factor Academy.

WHY FACTOR ACADEMY ALERT:
PLEASURE PAIN PRINCIPLE,

Some of the greatest teachers and thinkers throughout history taught us that avoiding pain is a more powerful motivator than the desire for obtaining pleasure. Your parents used it on you. If you didn't do a job, they would ground you. So the job became pleasure and the grounding became pain; so you did it. Unfortunately, I see in parenting that sometimes, the holding back of love is used to manipulate children. For example, if you don't do this... I won't love you anymore... this is destructive.

So, why is the understanding of this pain vs. pleasure principle so important to self-motivation? Because, by recognizing the principle, we can better control the direction of our lives by assigning the levels of pain vs. pleasure to the actions we are considering. In other words, you can operate your inbuilt program by re-programming your thinking, and by changing the pain threshold to a pleasure threshold.

Pleasure

There are many types of pleasure to be found in this world. Sometimes, pleasure involves success, but for some, there is a high degree of pleasure in being miserable. Think of people who can go on the dance floor for three or four hours. Once done, they aren't willing to walk 50 feet to the supermarket. Dancing was pleasure, walking was pain. This is a twisted sense of pain versus pleasure. Don't be a servant to pleasure only and be careful what you define as pleasure as it could really be pain. Because the pain can bring lasting pleasure. You have heard the saying "No Pain, No Gain!"

There are so many examples of how we get ourselves into trouble by seeking pleasure. For example, taking drugs seeking pleasure, leading to long term pain. Shopping, buying things to make us feel good, then have the long term pain of paying the debt off. So be careful, stop and think **is this short term pleasure or long term pain? Or short term pain and long term pleasure?**

Pain

It is important to remember that pain can be a very important part of success. **Without experiencing pain, you do not get the true meaning of happiness.** We need pain to know what pleasure really is. Pain can mean, 'I need to get out of bed.' However, we need to push through the pain of having to wake up early in order to become more successful. Once, I was so busy looking for pleasure that I did not deal with the pain of school in order to learn and become more scholarly. This made my journey more difficult, I fell behind, got the cane for poor results. School became pain and I left as soon as I could. In fact the pain of college was so much that when I left I did not want to do any studying or learning of any sort anymore.

The reason most people do not succeed is due to the fact that they visualise the change needed to be successful as pain. However, the successful people in the world override the pain threshold. They know the reality of the saying, no pain no gain. For instance, think of developing your body image at the gym. If you are overweight, you have to realise that you have a six pack under all that fat. You know it's there, but if you can't take the pain of gym training, diet, cooking and eating healthily, etc., you will never see the six pack. In life, you can live first class, second or third class. If you want to live first class, you need to be able to deal with a lot of pain initially, to achieve pleasure in the future. In other words there

will be sacrifices (pain) that you will need
to make and once you are prepared to do
that, then success is in sight. Does this make
sense?

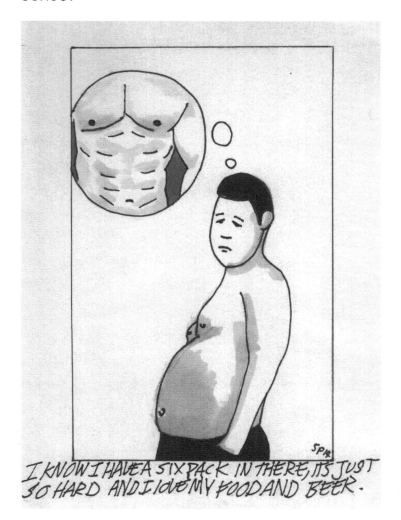

Moving from Pain to Pleasure

We are born with a *pleasure principle*, that we will seek immediate gratification of needs, for which our bodies reward us with feelings of pleasure. The reverse is also true, and the *pain principle* says that, whilst seeking pleasure, people will also seek to avoid pain. For this reason, we need to learn how to move from pleasure to pain, and pain to pleasure in a practical manner. To do this, we need to fully understand the origins of the Pleasure-Pain Principle.

The pleasure principle is at the base of hedonism, the idea that life is to be lived to the full and pleasure sought as a primary goal. Hedonists in the extreme will be self-destructive in their use of sex, drugs, rock and roll and other methods of gratification.

Pleasure and pain are the basic principles of Conditioning, where you get more of what you reward and less of what you punish. Pain can be more immediate than pleasure, leading us to become more concerned with avoidance of pain and hence paying more attention to it. This can develop into a general preference in life towards avoidance of what needs doing. That's why you hear people saying "I don't feel like doing that" because that feels like pain to them.

Anticipated pleasure and *anticipated pain* is almost as powerful a motivator as the feelings themselves, as we think about the pleasure and pain that may occur in the future. That's why, when you are embarking on a new project, the fear of failure knocks you down. It is arguable that these have had a significant effect on human evolution as they move us towards a more sustainable life. We live in a society today full of pleasure. In fact nearly every invention is designed to create pleasure and we will spend a lot of money to receive pleasure.

When pleasure and pain occur together, a certain amount of confusion may occur, which itself may be pleasant or painful and hence determine what happens. Simultaneous pain and pleasure is a basis for masochism. We are designed to move from what is painful to pleasurable. For example, we would rather go out and have fun, which is pleasurable, than stay at home and do our chores, which is not pleasurable.

Everyone Wants to Go to Heaven but No One Wants to Die

We all want the good things in life, but some of us are not prepared to make the sacrifices to get them. **We have instant coffee; we want instant success.** I remember someone who visited me at my home. I had a beautiful home with 14 acres of land, lakes, tennis courts, swimming pool. Even a five-hole golf course! They were admiring my home and they said to me that if they had a home like this, they wouldn't go to work but stay at home all day and play golf, tennis, relax and enjoy. I said to them, "keep dreaming, because if you did that, you would never have a home like this."

Successful People Override and Push both Pain

and Pleasure Thresholds

Successful people know how to override and push both the pleasure and pain thresholds. For example, if you want to approach your boss for a rise, you may imagine your boss getting angry or ridiculing you for asking. You associate the possibility of pain to them not taking the action. Furthermore, you assign a level or degree of potential pain to that action.

You may also imagine what a rise would mean to you or your family. You think of how good it would feel to have the additional money for something you want, or the pleasure you would feel providing something extra for your family. You associate the possibility of pleasure to taking the action. As with the potential for pain, you also assign a level or degree of potential pleasure to that action.

So, you weigh the possibility of pain you assigned to an unreceptive boss against the possibility of pleasure you assigned to what you could do with the extra money. Which one motivates you more? It's the one that gives you the most pleasure. Most often the fear of pain outweighs the hope for pleasure. So, you choose not to act. However, you have the ability to assign the weight of the pleasure and the weight of the pain to tip the scale. You can motivate yourself to ask for the raise by associating more pain to *not* asking for it, that's how you begin to re-programme yourself.

It is important to remember that we are instinctively motivated by *the need to avoid pain*. So, imagine and feel the pain you would experience by not taking action. Imagining the pain you would feel is your greatest motivator to take action. Then, as an added measure, imagine and feel the pleasure you would experience by taking the action and being successful as a result. Control the scale in your favour. Sometimes you are dealing with two pains; in this case we choose the less painful of the two.

Recognize that self-motivation is a choice you make. You can choose to motivate yourself, using the pleasure vs. pain principle, or you can allow your subconscious to control your actions by default. Don't allow your subconscious decisions to dictate your actions, or inactions. Ask yourself what is motivating you to do what you are doing throughout the day. Magnify in your mind the pain you will experience if you fail to act. Likewise, magnify in your mind the pleasure you will experience if you take the action that you know will ultimately be in your best interest. That's why it is important to have big goals; they activate your success mechanism and pleasure side. **All you have to do is turn the price you have to pay to succeed from the pain into a pleasure.** Then you will achieve your goal.

No Pain, No Gain

Successful people understand this. When I look back on my life, the years I spent struggling sleeping in an attic room, on the floor, in a car, on a friend's couch. Going to the shop and not being able to buy enough food for my family. I eventually turned this into the motivation to succeed. I made a plan to work, learn new skills and get out of my mess and commit to never go back. To enjoy a first class life. Why? Why Not Me? Why, Why Not You?

DARLING LOOKING BACK IT WAS WORTH ALL THE HARD WORK SEEING OUR CHILDREN HERE.

CHAPTER 11

MAKE A DECISION: WHY? WHY NOT ME?

n order to become successful in the Why Factor Academy, you not only need to ask yourself the question, Why? Why Not Me? but you also need to be genuine when you ask this question. You cannot simply say Why? Why Not Me? Instead, you need to make a powerful decision to make powerful changes in your life.

Beyond asking the question why? Why Not Me? you need to map your course of desired success. You need to set dates, goals and milestones. **First, you need to make the decision that you want to improve your life. Second, you need to make the decision of How to improve your life. Finally, you need to act on these decisions.** In this chapter, we cover what decisions you need to make, as well as how to start the process of proper decision making.

You Can Be Anything You Want To Be Within Reason

Within the Why Factor, it is important to remember that you can be anything you want to be in life. With this said, you need to have reasonable expectations within your life. For instance, if you are 50 years old, you cannot become a star football player in the Premier League. Instead, you need to set practical and reasonable goals. Having said that, you can be anything that you want to be. If you can conceive it you can achieve it, but it all starts with making a decision.

All Success Starts with Making a Decision

The path to success starts with a decision. For example, think about obtaining a driving licence. First we make the decision we want to drive, then we take lessons and persist until we pass the driving exams. To accomplish this, you need to take driving lessons, read books, and so on. In time, when we accomplish this simple goal, we can enjoy the freedom of the road. A great measure of simple success.

Another example. If you want to become a doctor, you first need to make the decision that you want to be a doctor and then accept you need to go to university for an undergraduate degree. Then, you need to move onto a more precise and difficult school of learning, medical school. If you decide you want to become a doctor at the age of sixteen, you need to realise the final goal is ten years away. However, this successful path starts with a simple decision. I want to become a doctor, so I must first get an undergraduate degree. An undergraduate degree is a great accomplishment. However, to become a doctor, you need to make a subsequent decision to go to medical school. First you decide you want to be a doctor, and then you go to college, university and do whatever it takes to achieve that goal. It's a long path, but a path which starts with an important decision. The greater the decision you make, the bigger the long term success will be.

Learn from the Mega-Successful

I always take time to learn from the mega-successful. I am reading the biographies of successful people, paying attention to their websites, follow them sometimes in the news, and so on. I like to listen to CD's and watch biography programmes of successful people, to learn what worked for them, and discover how I can apply what they have learned to my own life and business. Finally, as a modern method to learn more about successful people, I like to listen to podcasts whenever possible.

Beyond the person, I like to study their company. I like to look at where the company started, how the company grew, as well as the mission statements and actions of the company. For instance, I like to study how a certain company beats its competition to succeed in outlandish ways. I like to see how these successful companies and people deal with downturns, setbacks competition, and determine how they change from time to time, how they handle being more successful during certain quarters, and knowing when to accept losses when needed.

Lastly, I have found quotes to be a great way to motivate me, as well as explain the essence of a problem. Just not in business, but in life. A quotation is a great way to understand a very complex problem in a very easy way. For this reason, I like to listen to positive quotes from successful people and listen to educational and motivational CD's. You should understand that on a daily basis **making a decision to take action is the first step of success.**

MAKING A DECISION TODAY IS THE BEGINNING OF SUCCESS

MAKE A DECISION TODAY TO HAVE A HAPPY AND SUCCESSFUL LIFE

MAKE A DECISION TODAY TO LIVE A FIRST CLASS LIFE.

Why are you going to succeed?

What do you really desire? All great things start with a decision backed by great commitment.

Sometimes we make the right decisions; sometimes we make the wrong decisions. That is why we need to keep asking the *"Why?"* question, so we can capture it and reproduce it: and when we make the wrong decision, we can catch it quickly and make the necessary adjustments to put us back on track.

I learnt a long time ago that **most successful business people don't always make the right decisions but they always make their decisions right.** Once you make a decision it's like the universe coheres with you to deliver the result.

Examples of Decisions Successful People have Made

JOHN F KENNEDY

John F. Kennedy is a great example of a highly successful person, even though his life was tragically cut short. I love his vision in terms of the space race. He had a dream that one day man would reach out to the stars and the moon. He would actively seek to defy gravity, showing that man would not be confined to Earth.

In 1961, John F. Kennedy challenged us to turn our dreams into reality. This was his decision to commit. A true *commitment.* However, this dream did not happen overnight. Instead, it took the next 8 years to accomplish the goal of sending someone to the moon. The United States and beyond were inspired by his goals, dreams and aspirations. For this, the free world was organised and driven by one goal, to get to the moon.

In order to achieve his goals, John F Kennedy needed to assemble a team of over 500,000 people to land a man on the moon. The project required scientists, mathematicians, seamstresses, engineers, technicians, and so on to build the dream. New materials needed to be created, new means of communication, and most importantly, new ways of sending objects into space. Three individuals were selected to dedicate their lives to the remarkable mission. They too had to make a decision to put their own lives on the line for the success of the dream. On July 20, 1969, Apollo 11 landed on the moon.

Touchdown... The world was watching as Neil Armstrong put his first footprints on the moon saying, **"one small step for man, one giant leap for mankind."**

All because J. F. Kennedy made a decision.

ONE SMALL STEP, ONE GIANT STEP FOR MANKIND.

Roger Bannister

In 1954, Roger Bannister made a decision that he could run a mile in under 4 minutes. Everyone thought it was physically impossible, and that he would collapse and die if he ever approached such a remarkable time. But he **made the decision** that he could run a mile in under four minutes and did it in three minutes, 50 seconds, and his record only lasted for 46 days before it was broken. After he'd broken the barrier, many people went on to run under a four minute mile. So, in many ways, he did it when everybody said it couldn't be done. However, it was not luck which led to the four minute mile. It took lots of determination, belief and practice but most importantly, he made a decision it could be done.

This is an example again of belief overriding the pain threshold and then working at it until you get it. If we look at the current record for running a mile today, it is 3:43:13 seconds and it was set by Hicham El Guerrouj from Morocco. Now we live in a world where every year records are broken, even Olympic records are broken. Which record in your life are you going to break? Make the decision now.

Wright Brothers

The Wright Brothers said that they could build a machine that could fly and it led to them building the first aeroplane in 1903. The flight lasted 12 seconds and covered 120ft and from that decision, look at what we have today! Today, we fly around the world in 747's, 757's, airbuses etc., holding hundreds of passengers, we have space shuttles and satellites that make it easier today to explore the world and connect with people from all cultures. For this reason, we owe a lot to the Wright Brothers. Again they made a decision that it can be done. Think about it. All they had to go on was that they saw the birds flying and said, "We can do that!"

Berlin Wall

The Berlin Wall is a great example of how society can overcome great obstacles through hard work, determination and a dream. The wall came down because the people made the right decision to end communism. They chose to no longer live under the flag of tyranny, and because of this, the Berlin Wall came down in 1989.

Winston Churchill

Winston Churchill was a great leader. Why? Because he made the decision to stand strong and **never, never, never** give up. In one of his quotes he said, **"Hitler would have to break us or lose the war."** What a decision of strength and commitment. This is a great example of setting your Quit Ability Point up front.

YOU HAVE TO BREAK US OR LOSE THE WAR

Donald Trump

While Donald Trump is now known globally as a billionaire, his life was once very different. While he grew up in Forest Hills Gardens and was raised in a family with money, his fortunes once reached the point of bankruptcy. He took a risk which did not work out.

What separates Donald Trump from others is the fact he refused to give up. Donald Trump did not become a Why Me person; he was smart enough and worked hard enough to remain a Why Not Me person. At his darkest hour, Donald Trump was walking home and saw a beggar on the street with a few cents in his can. He turned to his wife and said, "you see that man, he is richer than we are right now'. But Donald Trump came back, he made a decision that he would rebuild even bigger, he learned from his mistakes and is now one of the most successful people on the planet. Remember, he lost everything, but he built his empire again. And so can you.

The Why Me sort of person would not have moved on to greater success like Donald Trump. For this reason, when faced with tremendous obstacles, you can never become the Why Me type of person. You need to make sure you can navigate your troubles correctly instead of caving into the short term pressures. In essence, you just need to make sure you do not turn into a Why Me person along the way.

Bill Gates

Bill Gates made a decision to drop out of Harvard College and, together with Paul Allen, start their own Computer Software Company. You know the rest of this story....

Martin Luther King

Martin Luther King was one of the leading figures in the Civil Rights movement and has had a defining influence on the history of the United States and the world. He made a decision to fight for what he believed in. Mr King delivered his famous speech in Washington on 28th August 1963 at the Lincoln Memorial. "I HAVE A DREAM that one day the promise of freedom and equality for all will become a reality." This legacy of equality is still growing to this day everywhere around the world. Why? Because King and many others made the decision to fight for what they believed in.

"I HAVE A DREAM"

Barrack Obama

Another great story from Martin Luther King's belief and decision, that one day we will all be the same, to Obama being president of the United States of America. Martin Luther King made a decision, Obama made a decision, "I can do this" and the rest is history.

Nelson Mandela

Nelson Mandela was sent to prison on the 11th June 1964. He refused three conditional offers of release and thirty years later, he was elected as the first democratically elected president of South Africa. When asked how he had coped with prison, Mandela said "I used it to prepare myself for when I would be released to lead and serve my country..." What a decision!

Richard Branson

Richard Branson has several stories he can tell you about decisions he has made, like how he made the decision to start Virgin Airlines with one plane and take on the big boys in the industry. Now look at Virgin Airlines and the Virgin brand today.

We have so many examples to learn from; it all starts with a decision. In short, make a decision today that no matter what happens, you will achieve. You are unstoppable.

Say to yourself now, I am unstoppable. Make a decision now and commitment that you and your family are going to live a first class life, for the rest of your lives!!

WHY NOT ME? I CAN DO THIS!!

CHAPTER 12

THE WHY FACTOR: 10 STEPS TO BRINGING IT ALL TOGETHER

What we have done so far is to clean your brain up, give you a mental shower, and get rid of the baggage, get rid of the thinking that's holding you back. Now we can start the process of building your success and realising the true potential in you.

213

To help organize your path to a successful life, I have created ten successfully established and easy-to-remember steps that I successfully used to train and develop many people. In this section, you will learn which steps you need to consider on a daily basis in order to achieve your goals. When it is time to reflect on your success, this list is a great place to start. Here, you can learn which factors you are excelling at, and you can learn which factors need more work. For this reason, make sure to always turn to this list when you feel you are slipping backwards.

The 10 Steps to Bringing It All Together: An Overview

1. Set Clear, Specific Goals

2. Believe in Yourself

3. Establish Your Quit Ability Point

4. Discover which Skill Level is Needed to Obtain Your Goal

5. Develop a Plan of Action

6. Work Ethic and Discipline

7. Building a Time Table for your Success

8. Accepting Feedback and learning from it

9. Accepting Full Responsibility for the Outcome of Your Goals

10. Fast Tracking Success: Listen, Learn and Apply

1. Set Clear, Specific Goals

The first step to success is to set clear, specific goals for yourself. You need to identify the steps you need to accomplish your goals, judge the time frames needed to achieve your goals, the costs of your goals, and so on. Remember, you can accomplish any goal, as long as that goal is within reason, within your belief system and you truly desire it. **Desire is the beginning of achievement.**

The first step to success is to set specific, clear goals; it's hard to hit a target that you can't see clearly. Decide today what you want in every key area of your life.

The main categories are: Career Goals, Personal and Family Goals and Self-Development Goals.

Career Goals- What do you want to do or be? What do you want to achieve? How much money do you want to earn a month, year or in 5 years time?

What job, business or position will give you the lifestyle you want? What job, career will give you the money that gives you the life you want, what status do you want to have?

Personal and Family Goals- What's your health goal? You have to accept responsibility for your health and that of your family. How can you improve the health of your family? What's your family goal? House, car, holidays you want to go on, school, college, relationship with partner, kids etc. what are your personal goal, what do you want for you, what gives you the greatest feeling of fulfilment?

Self-Development Goals- What do you need to do to achieve your goals? For example, discipline, time keeping, reading, motivational and educational books, CDs etc. What skills do you need to achieve your goals? What areas of help do you need? Who do you need to associate with to help you be a better and more successful you?

Make a list of all your goals. Review each one by asking "Why do I want this goal?" and "why is it important to me?" Go through each goal and categorise them into levels of importance, for example, A, B or C. Now you will have big goals, medium goals and small goals, in other words, A goals, B goals and C goals. Look for one or two big goals that will take out your small goals. For example, you want to earn £100,000 a year, in order to get the cars, houses and holidays etc., that you want. Go back to your A list goals and put a date you want to achieve them by. **A goal without a date is a wish.** Goals are what activate your success mechanisms. Make a list of your short term and long term goals and hold onto that list as we will use it later.

Also write each goal in detail, for example: under House, how many bedrooms? Garage? Pool? Garden? Car? Aston Martin? Which model? Which colour? What interior? etc. Your goals should be written in a detailed form that will allow you to visualize that goal clearly.

2. Believe in Yourself

Secondly, you need to believe in yourself. In other words, you need to have a positive system of beliefs; we discussed earlier the importance of this. To believe in yourself, you need to question your goals, you need to ask yourself if you truly desire the goal, why you desire the goal, what difference will it make to your life and ask the question of how important it is to you to achieve that goal. If your goals are not realistic, you won't believe in them. For example, you can't go from a £20,000 job per year to a £200,000 job per year in 12 months; your belief system won't accept it. You have to stage the increase from £20K to £50K, £50K to £100K, or £100K to £200K. Now I know people who have done that, but they are the minority rather than the majority. Most importantly, you need to believe in yourself that you can do it. Whatever you believe is true or false for you becomes reality. **Your beliefs are your control tower**. Belief is a foundation of every religion. In the Bible it says, "As a man believeth in his heart, so it is." or "Your faith will be done onto you." What you need to do is look at your goals, close your eyes and visualize your goals, believing as if you have already achieved them. **Once you believe in yourself and your goals, the sky is the limit.**

3. Establish Your Quit Ability Point

Remember, accepting failure and disappointment is a healthy part of your journey to living a successful life. With this said, you need to learn how to work harder when you feel like giving up. You need to establish early on what sort of pain you are willing to endure before you throw in the towel and quit. It is important to establish how hard it has got to be before you decide to quit, so that you don't give up at the first hurdle; use the pleasure-pain principle in your favour. So, make sure to ask yourself, what are the challenges you would have to overcome? Being honest with yourself, and setting reasonable expectations, will help you find the proper Quit Ability Point.

The Quit Ability Point is so important that you must set it up front on any tasks or goals that you would really like to achieve. Again, remember what Winston Churchill said: "They would have to break us or they lose the war." Another quit ability point that Churchill said was to **"never give up."** It's like going to the gym, if you make a decision that you will not quit until you get a six pack, then you will stay at the gym a lot longer. However, we go with no commitment and then quit shortly after. The Quit Ability Point gives you strength and power.

4. Discover which Skill Level is Needed to Obtain Your Goal

You need to discover what skill level is needed to achieve your goal. For instance, if you want to become a doctor, you can expect a lot of hard work, long hours and education. If you want to become a plumber or mechanic, you should count on spending time in serving an apprenticeship or going to college. In order to establish what skill level you need to achieve your goals, you need to spend time researching the path to your goals. A great way to do this is to seek out someone who has succeeded in your desired discipline. If you want to become a doctor, make sure to speak to a doctor about the time commitment, both while in school and after school. Make sure to paint a clear and realistic picture of your skill level, as well as the path to success. Again take your list of career, personal and family goals and self-development goals. Take the A list and ask yourself on each one, "What skill level would I need to obtain my goal?" You see, once you understand that it is a skill separating you from your goal, then you can learn, then you can achieve anything so long as you are prepared to put the time and discipline into learning the skill. Ask yourself **"Do I have the discipline to learn the skill that I need to succeed?"**

5. Develop a Plan of Action

You should now have an A list of goals you desire and believe in, with a Quit Ability point for each goal, the skill required to achieve the goal and a date you believe you can achieve it by.

With this in mind, take each goal and write it out on the top of a clean sheet of paper and develop a plan of action to encompass the details, dates, skills, research, quit ability point, etc. Write your plan as if you were writing a business plan and be careful who you share your goals and plans with. Share it with your spouse, a mentor, but no red people or Why Me? people please.

For example, I want a nice home. What type of home? 4/5 bedrooms, what size garden? What area do you want to live in, etc? All that information will give you a price bracket, then what you need to do is find out how much deposit you need and what your mortgage payments will be. Then you need to find a job/career to give you the income you need to get the deposit and qualify for the mortgage etc. You need a plan of action to get a job/career. Sales and business have always been great ways to increase your income and position, but there are so many other paths to increasing your income and that is what I mean by developing a plan of action. **A goal without a plan of action to achieve is worthless.**

6. Work Ethic and Discipline

Hard work is the best substitute for talent. Every successful person I know works hard and does more than 35 hours of work per week to begin with. My parents were quite influential when it came to building my work ethic as well as my positive and inquisitive attitude. When younger, my mother, a great teacher, taught me some powerful principles. She used to say, "If you are going to do a job, make sure you do it properly." She drilled this mentality into me. I was taught to always be hard working. This mentality helped me stay away from jobs and tasks which I knew I could or would never be great at. But when I identify a job I can do, I go after it and do not quit until I accomplish the goals of the job. Back your goals with hard work. **They say if you work hard enough you will get lucky.**

Most people know what they need to do but they are not disciplined to do it. It is important to understand that life is not about doing what you feel like doing but doing what needs to be done to get the job or task done. That's what successful people do, they do what needs to be done, and they override the pain and get it done, because they know the success lies just beyond the pain. This is discipline in action. Have you got the discipline to build a healthy, successful life for you and your family? Everybody has discipline but unfortunately some have it in the wrong areas so it does not amount to anything.

7. Building a Time Table for your Success

In order to be successful, you need to build a proper time table for your path to success. If you need to go to university, it is a good idea to record how long it will take to accomplish the goal, how much time you need to commit on a weekly basis, as well as understand what the vacation days are for the programme. This way, you can fill the void between terms with other goals you would like to accomplish. If you are not organized with your time, you are doomed to fail. For this reason, make sure to build a proper time table for your path to success. It is important to schedule the things that you need to be successful, otherwise they will never happen.

Again make a timetable from Monday to Sunday. Put in all the things you definitely have to do. If you have a full or part time job, write in all your hours to establish your free time availability to invest in your new project. You need to manage the work you have now and find time to build a business or the success you want in the future. Time management is the key. Another key process you need to do is to look at what you do now that you can stop doing or delaying to create more time to do the things you need to do. You can't keep adding to what you do now as there are only so many hours in the day. Remember when we covered the fact that there are only 86,400 seconds in a day. You have to use time wisely or you lose it. Successful people learn to use time and leverage it to build their successes. Prioritize your day, making sure your goals get priority every day; once your goal/work habits are committed to a time in your week. It will get done. Everything needs to be scheduled in the timetable; **I found in life that what gets scheduled gets done.** So take your detailed plan, dates etc. as discussed and make sure you apply them to your timetable. After a while it will become habit and you will be on the road to success. Make sure you allocate time in the week to reflect on your progress or lack of progress by asking "why is it working?" or "why isn't it working?" and especially, time for your family.

8. Accepting Feedback and learning from it.

Feedback is the breakfast of champions. Failures can also be great feedback for learning how not to do something. In order to succeed in life, we need to constantly review our progress by accepting feedback from others. Sometimes, the feedback comes from family and friends. Other times, feedback is best served by your boss or co-workers. Just don't settle for monthly or quarterly feedback. Instead, make sure to accept and seek out feedback on a daily, weekly and monthly basis. When listening to feedback, it is important to ask questions. Is this person qualified in what they are giving me feedback on?

For example, I remember when I started in Sales and my mother-in-law at the time said that I was wasting my time and I should "get a proper job." I am glad that I didn't listen to her, otherwise I would be working in a factory somewhere. You see when you stop and think about it, she never did sales; she didn't know anything about sales, so really she wasn't qualified to give me feedback. If you have plumbing problems you get a qualified plumber, not an accountant to fix it. One of the main reasons people fail is when they are about to do something, they get advice and feedback from unqualified sources. It amazes me how many people have opinions on sales but have never done it. Please do not listen! I never listened to anyone who wasn't qualified on what they are advising me on. Let me rephrase that, I listen to what they have to say but I do not take any action. You need to establish a small group of qualified people, mentors in the industry you are in and use them for feedback. Find a mentor, someone you believe in, trust and has been successful. **If you listen to failures, you will fail.** Wouldn't it be interesting if the failures held a seminar on how to fail, and who would go? You can give yourself feedback by asking yourself questions such as "Why Is It Working? Why Is It Not Working?" These are just two important Power Questions to keep in mind. Again ask your mentor, go to your boss and ask them why what you are doing is not working. They will appreciate you for your honesty and educate you. I hate to repeat myself but please get advice from qualified sources from people in the area you need.

9. Accepting Full Responsibility for the Outcome of Your Goals

One of the characteristics of successful people is that they accept full responsibility for the results. Most people confuse accepting responsibility with blame. **When you blame others or yourself, you look to the past and when you accept responsibility you look to the future.** We need to learn to take full responsibility for our actions, failures and successes. **Be a student of success and a student of failure.**

I'M STUDYING SUCCESS AND FAILURES.

I have watched people in businesses fail, I have studied them and seen where they have made their mistakes and then I've made sure I don't repeat them. Likewise, I study success, capture it and repeat it. It is simple when you know what to do. Once you accept responsibility for your success in life then there are no excuses; just learning curves and successes. This frees you to learn quicker. Accepting responsibility puts you 100% in control. How does that make you feel to know that you are now 100% in control of your life? **Once you gain control of your life you gain control of your happiness.** It's like you driving a car rather than being a passenger in someone else's car.

IT FEELS GOOD TO BE IN CONTROL.

10. Fast Tracking Success: Listen, Learn and Apply

The easiest way to become successful is find out what the successful people in your industry did to become successful and copy it. A carbon copy is only as good as the original, so make sure you have a good original. You don't need to be a good original but be a great copy of a great original.

The fast track to success in your life comes down to three simple factors: **Listen, Learn and Apply.** First, you need to make sure you listen to successful, qualified sources. Find a mentor who has been there, done it and succeeded in business and in life or in the profession you are seeking. Second, you need to make sure you learn and study this person, or persons or company, and their programmes and systems. <u>To earn more you have to learn more</u>. This is a key concept to success. Use audios, seminars, books, the Why Factor, etc., to speed up your success in the field you want to excel in. There is no excuse today with all the information out there, you have the world at your fingertips. Don't listen to music in your car or the radio, listen to educational, motivational CD's or MP3's. Turn your car into a university. Finally, apply yourself. Go to work, applying your learning to the world once you get the information from successful people. There is no substitute for practicing your skill to help improve your skill. **Knowledge is only powerful when you use it.** Simply put, just apply what you have learnt to your path to success. I like the Nike slogan, "Just Do It." Remember Winston Churchill said, "Never, never quit".

CHAPTER 13

USING THE WHY FACTOR FOR LONG TERM SUCCESS

To stay in control of your long term success by using the Why Factor is simple. Just keep asking yourself the Why question positively. Why is it working? Capture and repeat it. Why is it not working? Capture it, learn from it and avoid repeating the same traits. Use the Why question to drill down to the root of the problem and then solve it. **Your brain is an amazing machine**, once you ask it the Why question, it will find you the answers. The Why question will help you stay in control of your long term success and catch you quickly if you start drifting.

It can be hard to stay focused on your own. Find a partner or small group to work with who are on the same wavelength and goals as you. Use the Why Factor, training programs, etc. My mother used to say that two heads are better than one!

Power Questions

Power questions are questions that empower and move you forward. Ask these questions every day or choose a few to start with and watch yourself grow.

Commit to asking yourself each question ten times a day. Pick three to five power questions to start with, then work your way through. Have you heard the saying, how do you eat an elephant?... one piece at a time. Please take time to do the exercise slowly and write down the answers. What we are doing here is taking your thoughts, beliefs, etc., from your brain and putting it on paper. Once we have tidied it up, we can put it back into your brain. Now you own your thoughts and you are in control.

"Why" Power Questions

1. What are my special qualities and talents? Why?

_____

2. What will prevent me from achieving success today? Why?

_____

3. What makes me happy and content? Why?

_____

4. Why am I succeeding? Why?

_____

5. What's not working in my life right now? Why?

_____

6. What areas of my life would I like to change? Why?

_____

7. Why is... more successful than me? Why?

_____

8. Why am I not making the decisions I need to make? Why?

_____

9. What are my fears? Why?

_____

10. What's my biggest challenge? Why?

_____

11. What are my one year, three year, five year, and ten year goals? Why?

_____

12. What legacy do I want to leave behind? Why?

_____

13. Have I made a difference today? Why?

_____

14. What do I need to change in my life now? Why?

_____

15. Is my life in harmony? Why?

_____

16. Who do I love? Why?

_____

17. Who loves me? Why?

_____

18. What's my purpose in life? Why?

_____

19. What are my spiritual beliefs? Why?

_____

20. What can I do to serve society better? Why?

_____

21. What one skill if I had it would make a difference? Why?

_____

22. Do I like myself? Why?

_____

23. Do I have a great relationship with my parents and partner? Why?

_____

24. Am I a great role model for my family and business? Why?

_____

25. Do I have the respect and integrity from others? Why?

_____

The Why question can give you a positive or negative answer, either way you need to know. Just keep on asking the Why questions and use them to empower you because **now you have the Why Factor in your life. You will never be the same.** There are many more power questions you can ask yourself, please feel free to drop me an email with any other power question you discover and how it has empowered you.

ACTION! ACTION! ACTION!

Your Persistence is a Measure of How Much you Believe in Yourself and Your Goals

I want to thank you for taking your precious time and investing it into the Why Factor. I sincerely appreciate you and believe that, if you believe what you have read and make the decision today, yes today. Then you will have started the journey. A Chinese proverb says that, "a journey of a thousand steps begins with the first." The talk is over. It is now time to walk the talk. You are a Why Factor Academy graduate. You have 86,400 seconds to spend in a day - why not spend it on you? Discovering your potential, your abilities, enjoying the journey and enjoying life along the way. **You are like a light bulb waiting to be switched on, so you can light up the world.** It is now time to light the world up, make a difference and help others by being a role model of success and sharing your success.

IF YOU CAN FIND YOUR LIGHT SWITCH YOU CAN SEE

Hard Work Is the Best Substitute for Talent

Ladies and gentlemen, it is time for action, action, action! I would like to finish off with a story I once heard. Once upon a time, there was a cow that was happily grazing in the field. It was summertime and every day a bumble bee would come buzzing around the cow's face and ears, annoying her. So one day, the cow decided she had enough and that she was going to get rid of the bumblebee. So she came up with a plan that when the bumblebee came buzzing around, she was going to swallow it and that would be the end of it. So she started practicing, opening her mouth and closing it fast. Then the day came and the bumblebee was buzzing around her face and she quickly opened her mouth and swallowed the bumblebee. All of a sudden the bumblebee was in total darkness and was trying to figure out what had happened. The bee could smell a horrible smell and the bumblebee suddenly realised where it was, it was in the cow's stomach. It was so angry, it said, "That cow! That cow! I am going to sting that cow with everything I have got!" The bumblebee started thinking that this was going to be a big job, the biggest job it had ever undertaken. So as it thought about it, it thought that it needed to rest, get its energy up and when it woke up, it would sting the cow. So the bumblebee went to sleep, and when it woke up the cow was gone but the bumblebee was in the grass in a pile of... muck. And so it is, ladies and gentlemen, **If you don't take action now and you procrastinate, you will end up in a pile of... muck.**

IF YOU DONT TAKE ACTION NOW AND YOU PROCRASTINATE, YOU WILL END UP IN A PILE OF MUCK.

Today is your independence day, make a note of it.

My Independence Date

Date _____ Month _____ Year _____

You should by now be experiencing "Why?" fever. You should be asking yourself a load of why questions, don't worry in time it will all settle down.

Once again thank you for allowing me to be a small and important part in your life. I hope you have got at least one great idea from the Why Factor Academy that has or can change your life for the better.

Please join our academy and help the Why Factor Academy's mission to share the gift of health, happiness and wealth. We are on a mission to turn little people into big people and big people into giants. **Don't be on the outside looking in, be on the inside looking out. You should never question your ability but use the Why Factor to question your performance daily.**

I look forward to your performance equalling your ability. Why Not? Why not you? You deserve health, happiness and wealth.

Have a memorable life, believe in yourself and take action now.

Yours sincerely,

Ayo.

INDEX

**FOR MORE WHY FACTOR ACADEMY PRODUCTS
PLEASE GO TO: www.whyfactoracademy.com**